GIUSEPPE GARIBALDI

GIUSEPPE GARIBALDI

Herman J. Viola and Susan P. Viola

CHELSEA HOUSE PUBLISHERS
NEW YORK
NEW HAVEN   PHILADELPHIA

EDITOR-IN-CHIEF: Nancy Toff
EXECUTIVE EDITOR: Remmel T. Nunn
MANAGING EDITOR: Karyn Gullen Browne
COPY CHIEF: Juliann Barbato
PICTURE EDITOR: Adrian Allen
ART DIRECTOR: Giannella Garrett
MANUFACTURING MANAGER: Gerald Levine

Staff for Giuseppe Garibaldi:

SENIOR EDITOR: John W. Selfridge
ASSISTANT EDITORS: Pierre Hauser, Kathleen McDermott, Bert Yaeger
EDITORIAL ASSISTANT: James Guiry
COPY EDITORS: Gillian Bucky, Sean Dolan, Michael Goodman, Ellen Scordato
ASSOCIATE PICTURE EDITOR: Juliette Dickstein
SENIOR DESIGNER: Debby Jay
ASSISTANT DESIGNER: Jill Goldreyer
DESIGNERS: Laura Lang, Donna Sinisgalli
PICTURE RESEARCH: Toby Greenberg
PRODUCTION COORDINATOR: Laura McCormick
COVER ILLUSTRATION: Bill Tinker

CREATIVE DIRECTOR: Harold Steinberg

Frontispiece courtesy of The Bettmann Archive

3 5 7 9 8 6 4 2

Library of Congress Cataloging in Publication Data

Viola, Herman J. GIUSEPPE GARIBALDI

(World leaders past & present)
Bibliography: p.
Includes index.
1. Garibaldi, Giuseppe, 1807–1882—Juvenile literature.
2. Italy—History—1849–1870—Juvenile literature. 3. Italy—
History—1870–1915—Juvenile literature. 4. Generals—
Italy—Biography—Juvenile literature. 5. Statesmen—Italy—
Biography—Juvenile literature. [1. Garibaldi, Giuseppe,
1807–1882. 2. Generals. 3. Statesmen. 4. Italy—History—
1849–1870. 5. Italy—History—1870–1915] I. Title.
II. Series: World leaders past and present.
DG552.8.G2V555   1988   945'.08'0924 [B] [92]   87-14686

ISBN 0-87754-526-X

Contents

"On Leadership," Arthur M. Schlesinger, jr. 7

1. On the Road of No Return 13

2. The Adventurer.. 23

3. South American Exile..................................... 35

4. The Flames of 1848....................................... 47

5. Retreat to Fight Again 61

6. The Thousand... 77

7. Father of United Italy 95

8. Garibaldi in Retrospect 103

Further Reading... 108

Chronology... 109

Index.. 110

CHELSEA HOUSE PUBLISHERS

WORLD LEADERS PAST & PRESENT

ADENAUER
ALEXANDER THE GREAT
MARC ANTONY
KING ARTHUR
ATATÜRK
ATTLEE
BEGIN
BEN-GURION
BISMARCK
LÉON BLUM
BOLÍVAR
CESARE BORGIA
BRANDT
BREZHNEV
CAESAR
CALVIN
CASTRO
CATHERINE THE GREAT
CHARLEMAGNE
CHIANG KAI-SHEK
CHURCHILL
CLEMENCEAU
CLEOPATRA
CORTÉS
CROMWELL
DANTON
DE GAULLE
DE VALERA
DISRAELI
EISENHOWER
ELEANOR OF AQUITAINE
QUEEN ELIZABETH I
FERDINAND AND ISABELLA
FRANCO

FREDERICK THE GREAT
INDIRA GANDHI
MOHANDAS GANDHI
GARIBALDI
GENGHIS KHAN
GLADSTONE
GORBACHEV
HAMMARSKJÖLD
HENRY VIII
HENRY OF NAVARRE
HINDENBURG
HITLER
HO CHI MINH
HUSSEIN
IVAN THE TERRIBLE
ANDREW JACKSON
JEFFERSON
JOAN OF ARC
POPE JOHN XXIII
LYNDON JOHNSON
JUÁREZ
JOHN F. KENNEDY
KENYATTA
KHOMEINI
KHRUSHCHEV
MARTIN LUTHER KING, JR.
KISSINGER
LENIN
LINCOLN
LLOYD GEORGE
LOUIS XIV
LUTHER
JUDAS MACCABEUS
MAO ZEDONG

MARY, QUEEN OF SCOTS
GOLDA MEIR
METTERNICH
MUSSOLINI
NAPOLEON
NASSER
NEHRU
NERO
NICHOLAS II
NIXON
NKRUMAH
PERICLES
PERÓN
QADDAFI
ROBESPIERRE
ELEANOR ROOSEVELT
FRANKLIN D. ROOSEVELT
THEODORE ROOSEVELT
SADAT
STALIN
SUN YAT-SEN
TAMERLANE
THATCHER
TITO
TROTSKY
TRUDEAU
TRUMAN
VICTORIA
WASHINGTON
WEIZMANN
WOODROW WILSON
XERXES
ZHOU ENLAI

ON LEADERSHIP
Arthur M. Schlesinger, jr.

LEADERSHIP, it may be said, is really what makes the world go round. Love no doubt smooths the passage; but love is a private transaction between consenting adults. Leadership is a public transaction with history. The idea of leadership affirms the capacity of individuals to move, inspire, and mobilize masses of people so that they act together in pursuit of an end. Sometimes leadership serves good purposes, sometimes bad; but whether the end is benign or evil, great leaders are those men and women who leave their personal stamp on history.

Now, the very concept of leadership implies the proposition that individuals can make a difference. This proposition has never been universally accepted. From classical times to the present day, eminent thinkers have regarded individuals as no more than the agents and pawns of larger forces, whether the gods and goddesses of the ancient world or, in the modern era, race, class, nation, the dialectic, the will of the people, the spirit of the times, history itself. Against such forces, the individual dwindles into insignificance.

So contends the thesis of historical determinism. Tolstoy's great novel *War and Peace* offers a famous statement of the case. Why, Tolstoy asked, did millions of men in the Napoleonic wars, denying their human feelings and their common sense, move back and forth across Europe slaughtering their fellows? "The war," Tolstoy answered, "was bound to happen simply because it was bound to happen." All prior history predetermined it. As for leaders, they, Tolstoy said, "are but the labels that serve to give a name to an end and, like labels, they have the least possible connection with the event." The greater the leader, "the more conspicuous the inevitability and the predestination of every act he commits." The leader, said Tolstoy, is "the slave of history."

Determinism takes many forms. Marxism is the determinism of class. Nazism the determinism of race. But the idea of men and women as the slaves of history runs athwart the deepest human instincts. Rigid determinism abolishes the idea of human freedom—

the assumption of free choice that underlies every move we make, every word we speak, every thought we think. It abolishes the idea of human responsibility, since it is manifestly unfair to reward or punish people for actions that are by definition beyond their control. No one can live consistently by any deterministic creed. The Marxist states prove this themselves by their extreme susceptibility to the cult of leadership.

More than that, history refutes the idea that individuals make no difference. In December 1931 a British politician crossing Park Avenue in New York City between 76th and 77th Streets around 10:30 P.M. looked in the wrong direction and was knocked down by an automobile—a moment, he later recalled, of a man aghast, a world aglare: "I do not understand why I was not broken like an eggshell or squashed like a gooseberry." Fourteen months later an American politician, sitting in an open car in Miami, Florida, was fired on by an assassin; the man beside him was hit. Those who believe that individuals make no difference to history might well ponder whether the next two decades would have been the same had Mario Constasino's car killed Winston Churchill in 1931 and Giuseppe Zangara's bullet killed Franklin Roosevelt in 1933. Suppose, in addition, that Adolf Hitler had been killed in the street fighting during the Munich *Putsch* of 1923 and that Lenin had died of typhus during World War I. What would the 20th century be like now?

For better or for worse, individuals do make a difference. "The notion that a people can run itself and its affairs anonymously," wrote the philosopher William James, "is now well known to be the silliest of absurdities. Mankind does nothing save through initiatives on the part of inventors, great or small, and imitation by the rest of us—these are the sole factors in human progress. Individuals of genius show the way, and set the patterns, which common people then adopt and follow."

Leadership, James suggests, means leadership in thought as well as in action. In the long run, leaders in thought may well make the greater difference to the world. But, as Woodrow Wilson once said, "Those only are leaders of men, in the general eye, who lead in action. . . . It is at their hands that new thought gets its translation into the crude language of deeds." Leaders in thought often invent in solitude and obscurity, leaving to later generations the tasks of imitation. Leaders in action—the leaders portrayed in this series—have to be effective in their own time.

And they cannot be effective by themselves. They must act in response to the rhythms of their age. Their genius must be adapted, in a phrase of William James's, "to the receptivities of the moment." Leaders are useless without followers. "There goes the mob," said the French politician hearing a clamor in the streets. "I am their leader. I must follow them." Great leaders turn the inchoate emotions of the mob to purposes of their own. They seize on the opportunities of their time, the hopes, fears, frustrations, crises, potentialities. They succeed when events have prepared the way for them, when the community is awaiting to be aroused, when they can provide the clarifying and organizing ideas. Leadership ignites the circuit between the individual and the mass and thereby alters history.

It may alter history for better or for worse. Leaders have been responsible for the most extravagant follies and most monstrous crimes that have beset suffering humanity. They have also been vital in such gains as humanity has made in individual freedom, religious and racial tolerance, social justice and respect for human rights.

There is no sure way to tell in advance who is going to lead for good and who for evil. But a glance at the gallery of men and women in *World Leaders—Past and Present* suggests some useful tests.

One test is this: do leaders lead by force or by persuasion? By command or by consent? Through most of history leadership was exercised by the divine right of authority. The duty of followers was to defer and to obey. "Theirs not to reason why,/ Theirs but to do and die." On occasion, as with the so-called "enlightened despots" of the 18th century in Europe, absolutist leadership was animated by humane purposes. More often, absolutism nourished the passion for domination, land, gold and conquest and resulted in tyranny.

The great revolution of modern times has been the revolution of equality. The idea that all people should be equal in their legal condition has undermined the old structure of authority, hierarchy and deference. The revolution of equality has had two contrary effects on the nature of leadership. For equality, as Alexis de Tocqueville pointed out in his great study *Democracy in America*, might mean equality in servitude as well as equality in freedom.

"I know of only two methods of establishing equality in the political world," Tocqueville wrote. "Rights must be given to every citizen, or none at all to anyone . . . save one, who is the master of all." There was no middle ground "between the sovereignty of all and the absolute power of one man." In his astonishing prediction of 20th-century totalitarian dictatorship, Tocqueville explained how the revolution of equality could lead to the *"Führerprinzip"* and more terrible absolutism than the world had ever known.

But when rights are given to every citizen and the sovereignty of all is established, the problem of leadership takes a new form, becomes more exacting than ever before. It is easy to issue commands and enforce them by the rope and the stake, the concentration camp and the *gulag*. It is much harder to use argument and achievement to overcome opposition and win consent. The Founding Fathers of the United States understood the difficulty. They believed that history had given them the opportunity to decide, as Alexander Hamilton wrote in the first Federalist Paper, whether men are indeed capable of basing government on "reflection and choice, or whether they are forever destined to depend . . . on accident and force."

Government by reflection and choice called for a new style of leadership and a new quality of followership. It required leaders to be responsive to popular concerns, and it required followers to be active and informed participants in the process. Democracy does not eliminate emotion from politics; sometimes it fosters demagoguery; but it is confident that, as the greatest of democratic leaders put it, you cannot fool all of the people all of the time. It measures leadership by results and retires those who overreach or falter or fail.

It is true that in the long run despots are measured by results too. But they can postpone the day of judgment, sometimes indefinitely, and in the meantime they can do infinite harm. It is also true that democracy is no guarantee of virtue and intelligence in government, for the voice of the people is not necessarily the voice of God. But democracy, by assuring the right of opposition, offers built-in resistance to the evils inherent in absolutism. As the theologian Reinhold Niebuhr summed it up, "Man's capacity for justice makes democracy possible, but man's inclination to injustice makes democracy necessary."

A second test for leadership is the end for which power is sought. When leaders have as their goal the supremacy of a master race or the promotion of totalitarian revolution or the acquisition and exploitation of colonies or the protection of greed and privilege or the preservation of personal power, it is likely that their leadership will do little to advance the cause of humanity. When their goal is the abolition of slavery, the liberation of women, the enlargement of opportunity for the poor and powerless, the extension of equal rights to racial minorities, the defense of the freedoms of expression and opposition, it is likely that their leadership will increase the sum of human liberty and welfare.

Leaders have done great harm to the world. They have also conferred great benefits. You will find both sorts in this series. Even "good" leaders must be regarded with a certain wariness. Leaders are not demigods; they put on their trousers one leg after another just like ordinary mortals. No leader is infallible, and every leader needs to be reminded of this at regular intervals. Irreverence irritates leaders but is their salvation. Unquestioning submission corrupts leaders and demands followers. Making a cult of a leader is always a mistake. Fortunately hero worship generates its own antidote. "Every hero," said Emerson, "becomes a bore at last."

The signal benefit the great leaders confer is to embolden the rest of us to live according to our own best selves, to be active, insistent, and resolute in affirming our own sense of things. For great leaders attest to the reality of human freedom against the supposed inevitabilities of history. And they attest to the wisdom and power that may lie within the most unlikely of us, which is why Abraham Lincoln remains the supreme example of great leadership. A great leader, said Emerson, exhibits new possibilities to all humanity. "We feed on genius. . . . Great men exist that there may be greater men."

Great leaders, in short, justify themselves by emancipating and empowering their followers. So humanity struggles to master its destiny, remembering with Alexis de Tocqueville: "It is true that around every man a fatal circle is traced beyond which he cannot pass; but within the wide verge of that circle he is powerful and free; as it is with man, so with communities."

1

On the Road of No Return

Even on this fateful morning the man in dust-covered trousers and red shirt, sitting on a rock in the noonday sun, could well have been taken for a simple peasant tending his sheep. It was May 15, 1860; the place was a rugged hillside overlooking a valley near the town of Calatafimi on the island of Sicily off the Italian coast. The man on the rock, a black felt hat shielding his bearded, weather-beaten face from the sun, was no simple peasant. He had no sheep to tend. He was Giuseppe Garibaldi, an Italian patriot, and at that moment his attention was intently fixed on the opposite hillside, where thousands of soldiers from the Kingdom of the Two Sicilies were deploying for a battle that was to have a profound impact on the future of his nation. Among these troops milling about for position was his own small army of disheveled volunteers. As he observed the first chaotic throes of battle, Garibaldi knew that superior courage, rather than strategy, would win the day.

Except for its resemblance to a long, narrow boot with a ball-like island at its toe, Italy in 1860 bore little similarity to the country we know today. Not since the glorious days of antiquity, the days of the Roman Empire, had the Italian people been citizens

I am going into the unknown.
—GIUSEPPE GARIBALDI
before his departure for Sicily

The commanding figure of General Giuseppe Garibaldi embodied the spirit of the *Risorgimento*, a movement that united Italy in the 19th century. He remains the most revered and enduring national hero of Italian history.

ALINARI, FLORENCE

Garibaldi's volunteer forces defeated the regular army of the King of Naples at the Battle of Calatafimi. Their 1860 victory became a symbolic rallying point in Italy's struggle for unification.

of a unified country. Beginning with the barbarian invasions and continuing through the Napoleonic Wars (conflicts fought by French emperor Napoleon I between 1805 and 1814), Italians fell victim to one invader after another until, by the mid-19th century, their country resembled a vast jigsaw puzzle of city-states, dukedoms, and principalities.

As the country that had been the center of the Roman Empire and had produced the first flowering of the Renaissance following the Middle Ages, the Italian peninsula had sparkled with artistic brilliance, intellectual curiosity, and economic progress. Now Italy was little more than a pawn of three powerful political forces: the Austrian Empire, controlled by the house of Habsburg; the papacy, citadel of the Roman Catholic pope; and France, no longer the feared conqueror of Europe but still dangerous now that its Bourbon rulers again harbored visions of restoring their once vast empire.

Perched at the top of the boot, with France and Switzerland for neighbors, was the Kingdom of Piedmont, which, together with the island of Sardinia lying near it in the Tyrrhenian Sea, was known as the Kingdom of Sardinia. Modern Italy was to spring from this kingdom. The rest of northern Italy — the provinces of Lombardy and Venetia, the duchies of Parma, Modena, and Lucca, and the archduchy of Tuscany — was a possession of the Habsburgs. In the middle of the Italian peninsula were the Papal States, four provinces — Romagna, the Marches, Umbria, and Rome. These were con-

Proclaim to the Sicilians that now is the great moment to destroy the Bourbon regime, and we shall soon complete our victory.
—GIUSEPPE GARIBALDI

THE ILLUSTRATED LONDON NEWS PICTURE LIBRARY

A simple man himself, Garibaldi instinctively knew how to stir the hearts of Italy's masses to action. He was often pictured leading battle charges astride his famous white stallion.

trolled by the pope, whose authority over these territories was as absolute as any king's. The southern half of the boot was known as the Kingdom of the Two Sicilies or the Kingdom of Naples. Its ruler, the king of Naples, was a member of the Bourbon family, which meant that the region was Italian only in name.

To the inhabitants of these tiny jurisdictions, it made little difference whether their ruler was a pope, a Bourbon, or a Habsburg. Basically, they were all captive peoples with no political rights, no vote, and no freedom. Their lives, in fact, differed little from those of their forebears under feudalism, a system in which rich nobles owned the land and the peasants were serfs.

To many Italians such a situation was no longer tolerable. Indeed, for more than 40 years, the Italian peninsula had been seething with discontent. First one city and then another had been the scene of disorder, riot, and revolution as students, intellectuals, and radicals lashed out in desperation at their oppressors. Each time, a Bourbon, Habsburg, or

The Roman Forum, center of government in the time of Julius Caesar. Italians had not been citizens of a unified country since the Roman Empire's collapse in the fifth century A.D.

THE BETTMANN ARCHIVE

papal army had attempted to crush the spirit of the revolutionaries, only to see them rise up with renewed vigor somewhere else. Whether the uprising was in Venice, Rome, Naples, Milan, or any one of a hundred Italian cities, the revolutionaries had one goal, one hope — freedom from foreign domination and a united Italy. Their movement was known as the *Risorgimento* — the resurgence — and their military champion, the man who struck fear in all the monarchies of Europe, was Giuseppe Garibaldi, the dedicated patriot, nationalist, and revolutionary; and revolution was the reason for Garibaldi's presence at Calatafimi that fateful day in May 1860.

With Garibaldi were a thousand like-minded volunteers. Known to history as the Thousand, these volunteers were soldiers in name only. They were actually students, laborers, dockworkers, lawyers, doctors, and farmers who had flocked to Garibaldi's side from cities and villages all over the Italian peninsula. Like America's colonists-turned-revolutionaries in 1776 against their English rulers, the Thousand were filled with patriotic zeal, ready to sacrifice their lives to expel those who stood in the way of Italian national unity and independence. Their banner was the red, white, and green tricolor flag of Piedmont, which later became the flag of a

Rebellious residents of Paris hurled household items at members of the French Royal Guard during a raucous 1830 insurrection. The spirit of revolution spread throughout Europe in the mid-19th century.

Italian knights defend themselves against German knights. Since Europe's Dark Ages, Italy had fallen victim to one invasion after another; France and Austria were the dominant foreign powers in Italian provinces as the 19th century began.

united Italy, and their anthem was "Garibaldi's Hymn," by the composer Mercantini:

> To arms! To arms!
> The tombs are uncovered, the dead come
>   from afar
> The ghosts of our martyrs are rising to war
> With swords in their hands and with
>   laurels of fame
> And dead hearts glowing with Italy's name.
> Come join them, come follow O youth of
>   our land
> Come fling out our banner and marshal
>   our band
> Come all with cold steel and come all with
>   hot fire
> Come all with the flame of Italia's desire
> Begone from Italia, begone from our home
> Go from Italia, go from Italia
> O stranger be gone.

Anyone who can wield arms and does not fight is a traitor.
—GIUSEPPE GARIBALDI

They sang their hymn around their campfires, on the march, and as they paraded proudly through the villages and cities of Italy. They sang it as they went into battle, and they sang it at Calatafimi, when they struck their first blow for a united Italy.

As Garibaldi's citizen-soldiers moved into position, the Neapolitans on the opposite hillside had ample opportunity to observe them. They were not impressed by what they saw. Garibaldi's men had no uniforms, although many were wearing red shirts like their leader. Their weapons were obsolete muskets. Most of their guns might have been old and worn, but not their bayonets. These were new and brightly polished.

To the Neapolitan commander, Garibaldi's men looked like rabble. These peasants, he sneered, were the feared invaders? Enough time had been wasted on them. "Charge!" With trumpets blaring, the Neapolitans moved down the hill, splashed across the little stream at the base of the valley, and climbed purposefully toward the Thousand. It must have been a stirring sight — 3,000 infantrymen massed in formation, the buttons and buckles on their colorful uniforms flashing in the bright sun.

All the while the Neapolitans advanced, Garibaldi sat impassive. He ordered his men to hold their fire until the enemy was close enough for their antique guns to be effective — 100 yards at best. But Garibaldi could not control his eager men. A few armed with modern rifles began shooting at the Neapolitans and hit several. Seeing this, the rest of the Red Shirts suddenly leaped up and, with lusty shouts, charged down the hill, their bayonets at the ready. This the startled Neapolitans had not expected. They stopped, turned, and retreated to their original position, where, joined by fresh troops held in reserve, they opened fire on the advancing Red Shirts. Quickly the tide of battle turned. Greatly outnumbered and outgunned, Garibaldi's men faltered and then stopped. To escape the hail of bullets coming from the entrenched Neapolitans, the Red Shirts dropped to the ground and took refuge behind a series of garden terraces that marked the hillside like a set of stairs. The battle now turned into a stalemate, as both sides kept under cover, shooting occasionally when someone showed himself.

Now Garibaldi entered the fight. Although his men wanted him to stay out of danger, the old soldier refused to be a mere bystander. Down the hill he came, crossed the creek, and then began climbing the hillside. Several Red Shirts, fearing for their leader's safety, leaped up and stood in front of him to shield him from bullets; two were shot dead. Another officer, mounted on a white horse, galloped to Garibaldi's side. "General!" he shouted. "We should retreat!"

"No!" Garibaldi calmly replied. "Here we make Italy or we die."

Seemingly oblivious to the bullets whistling around him, Garibaldi pressed forward, moving steadily up the hill, past his men huddled against the hillside and behind rocks. The sight of the old man, sword in hand, challenging death, gave heart to his men, and they again began climbing the hill. Slowly, cautiously, a few at a time, they would rush from one terrace to another until, near the top, they were crouched behind the last one. Above them the Neapolitans, now only a few feet away, were firing as rapidly as possible at the Red Shirts. Few bullets found their marks, however, because Garibaldi's

Peasants of the foreign-ruled Italian provinces were essentially captive people with no political rights, no vote, and no freedom. Very few were even allowed to own land.

men were under the brow of the hill and the rounds were flying harmlessly over their heads.

The Red Shirts lay there for about 15 minutes. All the while, Garibaldi was moving among his men, encouraging them, telling them to rest before the last push. At the same time, the Red Shirts could hear the Neapolitan officers telling their men to move forward and sweep the Italian patriots off their protecting ledge. Had they done so, they would easily have overcome the 300 or so Red Shirts huddled on the ledge with Garibaldi. But they did not. Instead, frustrated at their inability to hit the Red Shirts with bullets, they began throwing rocks over the ledge. One bounced off Garibaldi's back. "They are throwing rocks!" he shouted. "They must be out of ammunition. Let's go!" Waving his sword, Garibaldi leaped forward, his men right behind him.

It was not ammunition the Neapolitans lacked but bravery. When the Red Shirts fell upon them, stabbing and swinging at them with their bayonets, the soldiers of Naples dropped their rifles and ran. Only a few moments later, the battle that seemed to be a crushing defeat for the rebels was suddenly turned to triumph. This victory at Calatafimi became a symbol and a rallying point for patriots throughout the whole of Italy.

In truth, the battle had been little more than a skirmish. No more than 30 Red Shirts lost their lives that day; perhaps another 100 were wounded. Neapolitan casualties were even fewer. The battle had an importance that far outweighed its military significance, however. Garibaldi had shown the world that Italians were willing to fight and die for their own freedom. It was a great moment for Italians everywhere. True, it was only the first step on what was to be a long campaign, but now there was no turning back. Leaving their wounded to be cared for by the people of Calatafimi, the victorious Red Shirts shouldered their muskets, and marching proudly with "Garibaldi's Hymn" on their lips, they proceeded on their history-making mission.

Ferdinand II, Bourbon king of Naples and the Kingdom of the Two Sicilies. The Bourbons envisioned restoring their once-vast French empire; Ferdinand's kingdom was therefore Italian in name only.

2

The Adventurer

I have lived a tempestuous life, and, as with most lives, it has been a mixture of good and bad," Garibaldi wrote in the preface of his memoirs. "I feel sure that I have always tried to act for the best both in regard to myself and toward others. If sometimes I have done wrong, certainly it was not with intent. I have always hated tyranny and lies, and am profoundly convinced that these two are the chief causes of the ills and corruption that affect mankind."

When Garibaldi wrote these words, he was in the twilight of his life. The simple statement is typical of this honest, humble man who seemed driven by the need to fight oppression no matter where he found it. Garlands were thrown at his feet, treasures and titles were his for the taking, but never did this selfless patriot seek wealth and honors for himself or his family.

Part soldier, part pirate, but all patriot, Garibaldi was a man of destiny. Even his birthday — July 4 — was appropriate for a great liberator. Garibaldi was born in 1807 in Nice, still an enchanting seaport on the Mediterranean Sea. At the time of his birth, this Italian city belonged to France, a victim of Napoleon's European conquests. Although later returned to Italy, it was given back to France in 1860, to which it belongs today. Its history was typical of Italian cities.

> *He was a professional liberator, a man who fought for oppressed people wherever he found them.*
> —DENIS MACK SMITH
> British historian,
> on Garibaldi

A harbor view of Nice, Garibaldi's birthplace. In his youth the future leader was headstrong and independent, characteristics that suited him well to the emerging revolutionary movements of his century.

The history of Nice was typical of many Italian cities: control of the rustic Mediterranean port frequently passed back and forth between France and the Italian province of Piedmont. Garibaldi first knew his hometown by its Italian name — Nizza.

Although Nice belonged to France, there is no question that Garibaldi was Italian, for his father, a sailor by trade, had moved there earlier from Genoa, the great Italian seaport. Domenici Garibaldi was a man of modest means who owned a small cargo boat that plied the waters between various ports along the Mediterranean coast. He fathered four other sons and two daughters, but only Giuseppe (Joseph, in English) lived to old age. This is somewhat ironic because Giuseppe, as a soldier and revolutionary, led the most dangerous life of them all.

Domenici Garibaldi did not want his son to follow him to sea. He wanted Giuseppe to have a better life than he had led, and he did his best to give his son an education, meager though it was. Giuseppe, however, was no scholar. He preferred hunting in the nearby hills or hanging around the docks. The sea was in his blood, and he could not turn away from it despite his parents' wishes.

As famous as Garibaldi became, few details of his

early life are known. He was an excellent swimmer, which was then unusual for an Italian. Although a great seafaring nation, few Italians ever learned how to swim. Young Garibaldi was also headstrong and fiercely independent, characteristics that remained with him for life. His stubbornness is reflected in an incident that occurred when he was about 15. Intent on going to sea, he and several friends stole a fishing boat and set sail from Nice, but they were overtaken before getting very far.

The theft convinced Garibaldi's parents to accept the inevitable. At age 16 he went to sea for the first time — as a cabin boy on a small trading vessel. He remained at sea, as ordinary crewman, first mate, and eventually a captain, for more than a decade. His skills as a seafarer stood him in good stead in later life, for they always provided employment and enabled him to make some hairbreadth escapes

The early campaigns of Napoleon Bonaparte had drawn all of Italy under the control of France by 1802. The French master painter Jacques-Louis David heroically portrayed the conqueror crossing the Alps into Italian territory.

Pirates claiming to be revolutionaries marauded the Mediterranean during Garibaldi's early years as a seaman. His encounters with them led him to claim it was "always better to fight when one is attacked."

when one or another of his revolutionary efforts proved less than successful. He also would learn to wage war at sea before becoming a master of guerrilla warfare on land. During the 1820s the Mediterranean Sea was a haven for numerous pirates, most of them claiming to be revolutionaries rather than ordinary buccaneers. Their victims usually met the same fate regardless of their political convictions or affiliations. The basic choice that faced ship captains who fell afoul of pirates was not a complicated one: resist, or surrender without a fight and hope for compassion. During one of Garibaldi's voyages into the Black Sea, his ship encountered pirates three times. Each time his captain offered no resistance; each time the pirates stripped the ship and crew of their valuables, the last time taking even the clothes off their backs. On his next trip into the area, this time with a different captain, they again met pirates, but the outcome was entirely different. This captain chose to fight. Although there were two pirate ships, Garibaldi and his shipmates successfully warded off the buccaneers. The incident demonstrated, Garibaldi claimed, that it was "always better to fight when one is attacked than to yield without a struggle." It was Garibaldi's first battle and the first time he was wounded, a slight injury to his hand. He did not realize it at the time, but he had just embarked on a new career.

During the 10 years Garibaldi was at sea, the intellectual movement of the Risorgimento swept the Italian peninsula. This spirit of unification, embodied in the movement, actually began in the late 18th century as an outgrowth of political liberalism fomented by the French Revolution. The dawn of liberalism promised freedom and a voice in government, hitherto unknown to Europe's populations. But to Europe's intrenched imperial leadership it meant only mischief and destruction. Whenever and wherever it surfaced, however, this movement was ruthlessly suppressed by the conservative rulers of Europe, led by Prince Klemens von Metternich, the Austrian foreign minister from 1809 until the revolutionary year 1848. For a time, his ingenious diplomatic maneuverings cemented the control of the dynastic empires in Europe through maintaining a "balance of power." His vision of European stability and order left no room for wars of national independence.

When Garibaldi was an eight-year-old child growing up in Nice, Metternich began drawing the boundaries of Europe following Napoleon's defeat and exile in 1814. For this purpose, Metternich orchestrated the Congress of Vienna in 1814–15, a momentous diplomatic gathering with decisive and far-reaching consequences for all Europe, but especially for Italy.

Through this congress, Metternich divided Germany and Italy, making certain that the Austrian Empire reaped most of the spoils. Both nations were deprived of economic and political unity. Thirty-nine separate principalities became members of a German Confederation, over which Austria presided until 1866. As for Italy, it had been reduced to a cluster of rival states as long ago as the early medieval period. Metternich's congress now aimed

> *His actions and daydreams show that he developed a conscious fixation and urge to be heroic, to deliver all victims of misfortune and oppression and make the world a freer and healthier place.*
> —DENIS MACK SMITH
> British historian, on
> Garibaldi as a young man

The Austrian prince Klemens von Metternich dictated new boundaries for Europe at the Congress of Vienna. His powerful political systems depended on the use of espionage, political and religious censorship, and the suppression of nationalist movements.

to make Italy's disunity a permanent reality.

Italy's partitioning was set forth in a "Final Act," the terms of which had been agreed to even before Napoleon's return from exile and last stand at the Battle of Waterloo. These arrangements of 1815 restored Lombardy and Venetia to the Habsburg rulers of the Austrian Empire. The Habsburgs also reigned over Tuscany and the neighboring principalities of Parma and Modena.

With the exception of Piedmont (part of the Kingdom of Sardinia), the north of Italy was in Austrian hands. To the south, the French Bourbon rulers were in possession of the Kingdom of the Two Sicilies (the island of Sicily and the mainland Kingdom of Naples). Pope Pius VII was placed once more in control of the Papal States. Only Piedmont remained an Italian state on Italian soil. It was the lone political base for building a unified Italian nation. Thus, "Italy," Metternich sneered, "is only a geographical expression." The Austrian foreign minister did not foresee that he was helping to create circumstances that would one day lead to a revolution against Italy's foreign masters.

Thousands of young Italian intellectuals and university students objected to Metternich's dismissal of their growing desire for an independent Italian nation. They began to form secret societies and to agitate for Italian freedom and unity. Students, infected with the revolutionary spirit, demonstrated their political beliefs by sporting beards, wearing their hair long, and smoking cigars. The police showed their displeasure by cutting the hair of some students, and throwing others in jail.

The strongest of the secret societies was the *Carbonari*, or "Charcoal Burners," who were so named

A meeting of the Carbonari, an antimonarchist secret society that flourished in Italy and elsewhere in Europe between 1785 and 1835. Members pledged themselves to support a romanticized version of revolutionary principles.

because they disguised themselves as makers of charcoal. Their guardian-overseer was Saint Theobald, who had been a charcoal maker. The Carbonari had been first organized against the French by Philippe Buonarotti near the end of the 18th century. The members pledged themselves to the revolutionary cause by signing their names in blood and espousing the motto "Despotism Annihilated." The society was widespread, claiming 50,000 members and appealing to visionaries and romantics throughout Europe. One of its most ardent supporters was the famous English Romantic poet George Gordon, Lord Byron, who once hid Carbonari weapons in his apartment. "I suppose that they

The British poet Lord Byron expressed the sufferings of Italy's political condition to the English public in his epic poem *Childe Harold*. He championed the cause of Italian independence by providing aid to the Carbonari.

consider me as a despot, to be sacrificed in case of an accident," he confided in his diary, but "it is no great matter, supposing that Italy could be liberated, who or what is sacrificed. It is a grand object — the very *poetry* of politics. Only think! A free Italy! Why, there has been nothing like it since the days of Augustus."

The person who gave the Carbonari intellectual vitality was Giuseppe Mazzini, a young student who became Italy's greatest political thinker of the 19th-century radical movement. Mazzini not only was an ardent patriot and nationalist, forming a group known as *Giovine Italia*, Young Italy, but he also had an international vision. He wanted patriots in all oppressed countries to rise up as one and overthrow the yoke of tyranny and autocracy.

Mazzini was also an activist. While Garibaldi continued to call at the ports of the Mediterranean Sea, Mazzini led one unsuccessful revolt after another — in Piedmont, in Naples, and in a score of other communities. Each one, thanks to the intercession of Metternich and his Austrian troops, was ruthlessly crushed. No longer did the alarmed authorities give the students haircuts. The lucky ones had their right hands chopped off; the others lost their lives. One of those executed was Ciro Menotti, a student from Modena. Garibaldi was later to name his first-born son Menotti in his memory.

Throughout this turmoil, Garibaldi was at sea, little concerned, little affected. In 1834 two things changed all this. First, his ship received an unusual cargo, a dozen political prisoners from France being sent into exile in Turkey. They were Saint-Simonians, named for a French freethinker, Claude-Henri de Rouvroy, Comte de Saint-Simon, who advocated, among other radical ideas, equality of the sexes and the liberation of women. Their philosophy was considered dangerous, and so many Saint-Simonians found themselves banished. Followers of Saint-Simon were opposed to the capitalist economic system well before another philosopher and economist, Karl Marx, began to criticize this system for its division of society into various classes, based on wealth. Proclaiming that "the golden age" was not over but,

Giuseppe Mazzini was among the greatest political thinkers of the 19th century. His Young Italy group split off from the Carbonari to espouse a radical nationalist movement, which Garibaldi soon joined.

rather, still to occur, Saint-Simon argued for a society governed by a committee of scientists and technicians. These unusually wise and learned individuals would ensure that the greatest good would be enjoyed by the greatest number. This last idea greatly appealed to Garibaldi, whose unwavering support for social justice remained a driving influence behind his military crusades. He could readily perceive unfairness and oppression and was ready to fight to end the wrongs he saw. But his thinking was somewhat muddled when dealing with the question of what form of government should prevail in an independent Italy. He was not at all certain that a republic, with its emphasis on political contests and parliamentary government, was appropriate. In subsequent years, Garibaldi's loyalty to the king of Sardinia and his own militant outlook inclined him to believe that Italians had "too much individual egoism." The Italian nation should be ruled by an absolute monarchy.

During the three-week voyage to Constantinople, however, Garibaldi befriended the Saint-Simonians and became intrigued by their ideas. "They proved to me," Garibaldi later wrote, "that the man who defends his country, or who attacks other people's country, is in the first example a virtuous soldier, and in the second example an unjust one; but the man, who becoming a cosmopolitan, adopts this second land as his country, and goes and offers his sword and blood to all peoples who are struggling against tyranny, he is more than a soldier; he is a hero."

The second event occurred shortly after the Saint-Simonians left his ship. At a seamen's club one evening, Garibaldi met one of Mazzini's disciples, who was exhorting the sailors to join Young Italy. The young man was so earnest and eloquent and so similiar to the Saint-Simonians in his convictions that he had little trouble converting Garibaldi to the cause. "I am sure that Columbus did not feel so much satisfaction at the discovery of America as I felt at meeting someone who was working for the redemption of our country." When Garibaldi returned to Nice after his cruise, he joined Young Italy and dedicated himself to the unification of his beloved nation.

Garibaldi joined in time to participate in still another of Mazzini's abortive attempts to inspire a full-scale nationalist revolution. His plan this time was exceptionally ambitious. He planned to invade Piedmont from Switzerland with an army of foreign revolutionaries. In the meantime, his men were supposed to have infiltrated the Piedmontese army and navy in order to stir up a revolution within the military. Garibaldi's assignment was to enlist in the Royal Navy of Piedmont and inspire the crew of his ship to participate in the revolt. The complicated plot was doomed from the start. Mazzini's numerically insignificant invasion force was easily driven off, while loyalist soldiers and sailors revealed the plans of the revolutionaries to the military authorities. Most of the infiltrators were arrested. Mazzini escaped to England; Garibaldi, disguised as a peasant, escaped to Nice, where he learned that he had already been condemned to death and would be executed should he be captured by Piedmontese authorities. He had no recourse but to flee Italy. Saying good-bye to his parents — he never saw his father again — he slipped into France, where he joined other disillusioned revolutionaries like himself. Garibaldi remained an exile from his homeland for the next 14 years.

3

South American Exile

The decade and a half Garibaldi spent away from Italy was important to his development as a soldier and revolutionary. During this time, he kept uppermost in his mind his goals for the unification of Italy, and he remained in touch with the leaders of the Risorgimento.

The first stop on his 14-year odyssey was the French seaport of Marseilles, where he arrived in the spring of 1834. To support himself, he returned to the sea, signing on as a crewman on board a French cargo ship that operated between Marseilles and the Levant. When his ship returned to Marseilles, he found the city in the grips of a cholera epidemic. This dreaded disease had no cure, and the citizens were so afraid of contracting it that there were not enough people to tend the sick and dying. Garibaldi, however, answered the appeals for volunteers and spent some two weeks driving ambulances and working in hospitals. This selflessness is so typical of the remarkable revolutionary that some biographers speculate that, under different circumstances, Garibaldi could easily have become an Italian saint.

After a year in Marseilles, Garibaldi left for South America. His motive for this dramatic move is unknown, but he probably did it for no more profound reason than to see another part of the world. All this time he had been in France illegally, using an as-

> *Here he learned to live hard, free as the air, a law to himself in a land where nature was cruel and life was cheap.*
> —DENIS MACK SMITH
> British historian,
> on Garibaldi in
> South America

A portrait of Garibaldi painted in Uruguay during his 14-year exile. His goal of a united Italy remained uppermost in his mind even while he fought valiantly for other nationalist causes in South America.

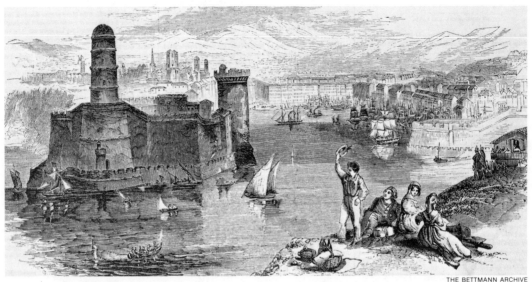

Garibaldi spent his first year of exile illegally in the French seaport of Marseilles. His willingness to assist victims of a cholera epidemic there was typical of his selfless concern for others.

sumed name, and perhaps he felt it was time to make a new life for himself. Certainly Garibaldi was not alone in his decision. Thousands of Italians had already emigrated to South America to escape the repression of western Europe, and large communities of Italian exiles could be found in several Latin American cities. Garibaldi chose to go to Rio de Janeiro, where he arrived in November 1835. To finance his passage, he had signed on as a crewman on a French ship, using the alias Giuseppe Pane.

Garibaldi found South America gripped by the same revolutionary fervor he had left in Europe. Spain and Portugal had divided South America into colonial possessions in the same repressive manner that the dominant royal families controlled Europe. Even if he had wanted to escape the excitement of revolution, Garibaldi would have been hard-pressed to do so in South America.

Almost as soon as he arrived, Garibaldi resumed his role as a patriot and activist. His first step was to join the Rio chapter of Young Italy, headquartered in a house over which was flown the green, white, and red flag intended for the future Republic of Italy.

Garibaldi's first task was to write articles attacking the Kingdom of Sardinia, but letter writing soon became tedious to the born adventurer. Writing to

Mazzini, he offered to become a privateer in the name of Young Italy and attack Austrian and Sardinian ships that visited Brazilian ports. Even Mazzini rejected this reckless idea. Thus, instead of becoming a pirate, Garibaldi entered the food business, carrying macaroni between Rio and Cabo Frio. He named his ship the *Mazzini* and flew the Italian tricolor flag. Garibaldi was rescued from this humdrum occupation by a revolution that broke out in Brazil's Rio Grande do Sul, a southern region adjoining Uruguay and Argentina. The revolutionaries, whose ideas bore a striking resemblance to those of the Risorgimento, appealed to Garibaldi and other Italians living in Brazil, and many of them joined the revolution. Here was Garibaldi's chance to become a privateer.

It was a dangerous move, for most people viewed privateers as little more than pirates, and Garibaldi had a small ship and only a few crewmen. In his first fight with a Brazilian warship, he was almost

A street in the Brazilian city of Rio de Janeiro, where Garibaldi arrived in 1835. The South American colonies were as ripe for revolt against their repressive overlords as the European subject-states Garibaldi had left.

killed by a bullet that struck him in the neck. Although his ship escaped to Argentina, Garibaldi took three months to recover fully from his wound. Undaunted, he continued his war against Brazil, sometimes over land, sometimes by sea. During this time he came in contact with rebel cavalry. Much like the cowboys of the American western frontier, the rebel *gauchos* wore a distinctive costume and literally lived on horseback. Considered among the finest horsemen in the world, the fearless gauchos could make lightninglike strikes against superior forces and then easily elude their pursuers. They lived off the land, butchering and roasting cattle, using lassos as readily as guns. They were so tough they could remain in the field for weeks at a time, traversing immense distances. The principles of guerrilla warfare that Garibaldi learned from these brave and hardy horsemen were to make him equally as feared when he returned to the battlefields of Europe. The gauchos so impressed Garibaldi that he adopted their dress. For the rest of his life, he wore their distinctive poncho and loose-fitting clothing.

Argentina's rebel cavalry was made up of fearless horsemen called *gauchos*, who could fight for weeks at a time while living off the land. Garibaldi absorbed many of their principles of guerrilla warfare.

For three years Garibaldi was involved in the revolutionary movements of the region. Fighting occurred not only in Brazil but also spilled over into neighboring Argentina and Uruguay. In this warfare, which involved small units, sporadic skirmishes, and therefore fewer casualties, Garibaldi began earning a reputation as a forceful leader and gifted strategist. Surely one of his most spectacular achievements was the cross-country transportation of ships so they could participate in a combined land and sea strike against the Brazilian town of Laguna, a small port on the Atlantic coast. The feat was accomplished by one of Garibaldi's men, a clever engineer, who designed a cart that could be placed under the vessels while they were in water. Then, with the aid of 200 oxen, Garibaldi was able to pull the ships a distance of 50 miles over land to the Atlantic Ocean, where they put to sea.

Unfortunately, soon after being re-placed in the ocean, a severe storm swamped one of the boats. Of the 30 crewmen, more than half drowned, including some of Garibaldi's closest friends. Loss of the ship did not impede the attack, however. Garibaldi was given another ship, and the assault proceeded as planned. It was a stunning victory for the rebels and enhanced Garibaldi's reputation even more.

Iguaçu Falls, between Argentina and Brazil in the Rio Grande do Sul province. Many Italians living in Brazil joined the region's revolutionary movement; Garibaldi went back to sea as a coastal privateer running supplies for the rebels.

DAVID LEES, FLORENCE

Garibaldi's poncho was well used both as cloak and as blanket. The practical abilities of the gauchos so impressed Garibaldi that he adopted their loose-fitting, distinctive clothing for the rest of his life.

Many are the stories of her courage, her endurance, and her fierce jealousy.
—DENIS MACK SMITH
British historian, on
Anita Garibaldi

Using Laguna as a base, Garibaldi continued to harass Brazilian shipping along the Atlantic coast. These were unhappy days for the exiled Italian, however. He felt deeply the loss of his friends and often was overtaken by fits of melancholy. It was in this frame of mind that Garibaldi, as his ship was entering the Laguna harbor after one of his raids, spied a beautiful girl on a distant hillside. As soon as he docked his ship, he went to the spot where he had seen her through his telescope. When he got there, she was gone. While searching the neighborhood for her without success he met one of the townsfolk, a casual acquaintance, who invited him home for a cup of coffee. Imagine Garibaldi's shock and surprise when the woman who brought them their coffee turned out to be the girl on the hillside. "We both remained enraptured and silent," Garibaldi recalled. "We gazed on each other like two people who had met before, and seeking in each other's faces something which makes it easier to recall the forgotten past."

"You must be mine," he stammered in broken Portuguese.

This is how Garibaldi met Anita, the woman who was to be his constant companion for just short of a decade. She must have been a remarkable person, for she shared his life completely. She rode at his side on raids against his enemies, cooked his food, and bore his children; she became a symbol to increasing numbers of women who treasured the hope of one day achieving complete political and social equality for their sex. "She was no less zealous," Garibaldi boasted, "than myself for the sacred cause of nations and for a life of adventure."

Although she was an important part of Garibaldi's life, facts about Anita are obscure. Some historians have suggested that Anita Ribeiro da Silva, only 18 when she fell in love with the dashing and romantic corsair, may well have been married already. This point may never be satisfactorily resolved, but despite its truth or falsity, Anita remained faithful to Garibaldi until her tragic death.

Soon after their elopement, the fortunes of war turned against the rebels. Anita herself was captured after one engagement. When her captors told her Garibaldi was among the dead, she searched the battlefield for him, turning over bodies and examining each face. He had eluded death, however, and she was determined to join him. That night she escaped, and after a remarkable four-day journey on foot and horseback, she found Garibaldi safe and unharmed in a small village some 70 miles from the battlefield.

For Garibaldi and his men there followed a retreat of some 450 miles, marked by constant fighting and constant running. Of this period of danger and high adventure, Garibaldi recalled in his memoirs, "I had a sword and carbine, which I carried before me

Garibaldi's first wife, Anita. The romance of their initial meeting set the tone of their life together; he loved her at first sight and inspired in her a passionate commitment to independence causes that rivaled his own.

across the saddle. Anita was my treasure, and no less zealous than myself for the sacred cause of nations . . . and the hardships of camp-life as a pastime; so that, however things might turn out, the future smiled on us, and the vast American deserts that unrolled themselves before our gaze seemed all the more delightful and beautiful for their wildness."

Meanwhile, Anita became pregnant, and Garibaldi's first son, Menotti, was born in September 1840. That year the Garibaldi family seldom had a moment's peace and virtually lived in the saddle, for the imperial forces kept them continually on the run. How the baby survived those early months is a mystery. On one occasion, while attempting to cross mountains, Garibaldi kept the infant in a sling against his chest.

This was no life for a family man, Garibaldi realized, and a few months after Menotti was born he moved to Montevideo, Uruguay, where he and Anita were married and he attempted to adjust to a life of domestic peace. In this he was singularly unsuccessful, even though he tried his hand at a variety

Garibaldi's elaborately tooled saddle from his years in South America is preserved in the Museum of the Risorgimento, Rome.

A popular likeness of Garibaldi from South America. His Italian Legion of expatriates gained international acclaim for their pivotal role in securing Uruguay's independence from Argentina; some of those legionnaires followed him back to Italy to lead the Risorgimento.

of domestic pursuits, including teaching. Once again fate rescued him from an ordinary life when Argentine soldiers invaded Uruguay. Garibaldi accepted a commission in the Uruguayan navy, a military force that existed largely on paper.

Not only was he responsible for organizing Uruguay's navy; Garibaldi conceived and established the Italian Legion. This was a force made up of expatriate Italians, like himself, who were to band together for the sake of fighting for Uruguayan independence, if unable to do so for their own homeland. The legionnaires were remarkably successful, so much so that the Argentines were unable to cap-

Once again it is hard to see quite what was at issue in this particular war. But Garibaldi did not investigate the situation too closely, and soon managed to believe that he was fighting for humanity and liberty in general.
—DENIS MACK SMITH
British historian,
on Garibaldi
in Uruguay

ture Montevideo despite a lengthy siege. Garibaldi was so essential to the defense of Uruguay that the Argentines eventually tried to purchase his loyalty. "You should try to win the *gringo* Garibaldi, who is the inspiration of the savage Unitarians [rebels] besieged in Montevideo, without stinting the amount," wrote one Argentine official to his field commander. "I have used all possible means to achieve this" was his exasperated reply, "but he cannot be won [through bribery]; he is a stubborn savage."

Few of the legionnaires were professional soldiers. Most were civilians fighting in defense of the country that had given them sanctuary. They were unpaid, and their only uniform was a red shirt, which became their symbol and their glory. The shirts were chosen because Garibaldi had sought the most inexpensive materials in outfitting his men. The red shirts had been ordered for use in the Argentine cattle industry. The red did not show the blood when worn by workers in the slaughterhouses. Be-

"La Sentinella Garibaldina" portrays a young sentry standing watch for the Italian Legion. He wears a simple red shirt, the uniform that gave Garibaldi's men their famous nickname.

cause of the war the shirts were undeliverable, so the Uruguayan government got them at a cheap price and issued them to the Italian Legion.

Because the red woolen shirts were bulky, the soldiers usually wore them loosely over their trousers. For overcoats, Garibaldi chose the equally inexpensive and practical woolen poncho worn by the gauchos, who used it as both cloak and blanket.

With their distinctive uniform and their humble but romantic leader, the Italian Legion quickly gained international admirers. The people of Italy, especially, followed their activities with pride and the hope that one day the legionnaires — with their jaunty red shirts and black flag, a volcano in the center (symbolizing the sacred fire of freedom in the heart of Italy) — would help their own countrymen fight for freedom.

Garibaldi, meanwhile, had not forgotten his native land. As the years passed, he became more impatient to take up once again the cause of Italian unification. And, despite his almost ceaseless campaigning, his family continued to grow. Menotti was followed by a daughter, Rosita, who died of scarlet fever; another daughter, Teresita; and another son, Ricciotti, named for an Italian patriot executed in Naples in 1844.

Throughout the Uruguayan war, Garibaldi never lost his awareness of the plight of the people of Italy. He kept in touch with his friends, former revolutionaries still at home, and he corresponded with Mazzini, still biding his time in London. Finally, in 1848, Garibaldi decided to return.

Ricciotti, like Garibaldi's other sons born during the exile, was named for a martyred Italian patriot. After more than a decade of championing other causes, Garibaldi yearned to return home and exploit his hard-won fighting skills for the sake of Italian freedom.

4

The Flames of 1848

The year 1848 shook the royal houses of Europe with revolution. Virtually no nation on the continent was left untouched by political unrest. At the epicenter of revolt were three countries: France, Austria, and Italy. The Second Republic arose in France, having driven from power King Louis-Philippe. Emperor Franz Joseph II of Austria ascended the throne amid rioting in Vienna. Piedmontese king Charles Albert (father of Victor Emmanuel II) tried using certain reforms to fend off the threat of revolt among his people against the occupying Austrians. Students, intellectuals, and other liberals found common cause in their attempt to overthrow the conservative monarchies of Europe, which continued to deny individual rights and stifle the feelings of nationalism that blazed in the hearts of their subject peoples.

While the spirit of liberation reached a flash point throughout the Habsburgs' vast empire, nowhere did it burn more fiercely than in Italy. As early as 1844, after a 10-year period of relative inactivity, Mazzini and his followers attempted once again to lead a popular uprising. The target this time was Calabria, at the toe of the Kingdom of the Two Sicilies. The peasants refused to join the revolutionaries who landed there, and eventually they were all captured. Nine were executed, including Nicola Ricciotti, the young man for whom Garibaldi named

> *The revolutions of 1848 should have given the Concert of Europe a new lease on life by warning the princes of the developing threats to their authority and of the greater need for unity and vigilance.*
> —NORMAN RICH
> American historian

Garibaldi in 1849, when he led the Roman Republic's armed defense of Rome against the French. Although Rome ultimately fell, his stirring leadership established him as the undisputed hero of Italian nationalism.

The election of Pius IX as pope in 1846 led to an outburst of liberal enthusiasm. *Pio Nono*'s voluntary political reforms spurred Garibaldi's decision to return to Italy even though his death sentence was still in effect.

The Roman Pontiff can and ought to reconcile himself, and come to terms, with progress, liberalism, and modern civilization.

—POPE PIUS IX

his second son. Their deaths nevertheless served as an inspiration to revolutionaries everywhere. In the face of the firing squad they defiantly sang: "He who dies for his country has lived long enough."

The situation in Italy was so volatile that Pope Pius IX, elected in 1846, decided to liberalize life in the Papal States. He freed political prisoners, repealed laws against Jews, abolished persecution of heretics, and established a legislative council for the city of Rome, with some of the members elected by the people.

The pope's mild reforms encouraged liberals throughout the peninsula, who wished to see similar steps taken in other Italian states. Indeed, they hoped the pope, Pius IX, whom they called Pio Nono, would lead the movement to drive out the French and Austrian rulers who still controlled so much of the country. And one of those who offered to help the pope in this effort was Garibaldi. "If these hands, which are used to fighting, would be acceptable to His Holiness," he wrote from Uruguay in October 1847, "it is unnecessary to say that we dedicate them most willingly to the service of him who has done so much for our country and the Church. We would be happy indeed if we could cooperate in Pius IX's work of redemption . . . and we do not think that we would pay too high a price if it costs us our blood."

The pope rejected the offer. Garibaldi nevertheless believed that the time had come for him to return to Italy. In January 1848 he sent Anita and their children to Nice to live with his mother. Accompanied by the wives and children of other legionnaires, she left South America, never to return. Garibaldi himself remained in Uruguay a few months longer, for his departure required some planning. Still under a death sentence in Italy, he needed to enter the country secretly, and this required a ship of his own, which he bought by raising money from Italians living in Montevideo.

He renamed his small ship the *Speranza* — Hope — and left for Italy on April 14. With him sailed 63 of his Red Shirts. Most of them were seasoned combat veterans as well as zealous patriots, and most of them were destined to die on the battlefields of Italy. Perhaps the most remarkable of his legionnaires was a tall and muscular black man from Brazil named Aguiar, who was Garibaldi's friend as well as protector.

During the two months that the *Speranza* was at sea, a revolutionary signal electrified Europe. One of the bloodiest revolts took place in the Italian city of Milan, where Metternich's Austrian troops took several days of bitter street fighting to crush the uprising. To the Milanese, the revolt became known as "The Five Glorious Days." Revolution was in the air, and Garibaldi — his death sentence forgotten — was never to receive a more rousing welcome. When Anita arrived in Nice, she was treated like a heroine. Cheering crowds welcomed her with shouts of "Long live Garibaldi! Long live Garibaldi's family!" Her welcome, however, was nothing compared to the tumultuous reception that awaited Garibaldi and his Red Shirts when they arrived several weeks later.

Despite his 14-year absence from home, Garibaldi did not tarry long in Nice. "There is fighting to do," he told Anita and his widowed mother. Bolstered by an additional 100 volunteers who had joined his legionnaires upon their arrival, Garibaldi left for Piedmont, where he offered his services to King Charles Albert, who was then fighting the Austrians in the neighboring states of Lombardy and Venetia.

But Charles Albert did not want help. He had already turned down offers of assistance from France with the comment *"Italia farà da sè"* ("Italy will do it alone"). And, perhaps fearing Garibaldi's republican sentiments, he rejected the aid of the Red Shirts. "To make such a man a general would be dishonoring to the enemy," the king scoffed. It was a foolish decision. On July 24 the Austrians, although outnumbered, soundly defeated the forces of Charles Albert at the Battle of Custozza. Garibaldi, meanwhile, had gone to Milan, where he was appointed a general in the Lombard army and organized a force of 1,500 men. With this little army, Garibaldi planned to wage his own war against the Austrians, but Charles Albert completely reversed the situation by signing a truce with them.

Garibaldi's widowed mother received her son's first visit on his return to Italy in 1848. He described her in his autobiography as "my aged mother, whom I loved almost to idolatry, and had not seen in fourteen years."

Garibaldi and Aguiar, a black Brazilian rebel, on horseback. The remarkable Aguiar (left) was Garibaldi's friend as well as protector; he was 1 of the 63 Red Shirts who accompanied their leader to Italy from South America.

The armistice infuriated Garibaldi, who considered it a treacherous act by a monarch who wished to save his throne while sacrificing the hopes of Italy's freedom fighters. Convinced that he could no longer work with the rulers of the Italian states, Garibaldi decided to bring his case to the Italian people. On August 13, 1848, he issued his famous Castelletto Manifesto: "Chosen in Milan by the People and their representatives as leader of my men, with no aim except that of Italian independence, I am not able to conform to the humiliating convention which has been signed by the King of Sardinia with the hated foreigner dominating my country. If the King of Sardinia has a crown which he wishes to save by guilt and cowardice, my companions and I do not wish to save our lives by infamy, and to abandon, without sacrificing ourselves, our sacred soil to the mockery of those who oppress and ravage it."

Garibaldi's manifesto established him as a national hero and revived the morale of the common people throughout the country, but it failed to inspire a national uprising. This statement became a cornerstone of the movement — and its handful of ideas — sometimes called *Garibaldinismo*. Undaunted, he moved into the mountains of northern Italy and waged a guerrilla war against the hated Austrians. He did engage in a few violent skirmishes, but for the most part his activity had little impact on the unification effort, even though Mazzini joined him for a time. In fact, it had the opposite effect, because Mazzini and Garibaldi quarreled over the best way to achieve their goal. Mazzini thought Garibaldi had been wrong to offer his services to Charles Albert, who represented the forces of autocracy and repression; Garibaldi chided Mazzini for being too idealistic and told him he would ally himself with anyone if it would further the cause of Italian unification. Their collaboration lasted only a short time; then each went his separate way: Garibaldi to Nice, for a reunion with his family; Mazzini to Rome, where he played a major role in events that were to bring the two great revolutionaries together again more quickly than either had expected.

Although Pio Nono had instituted liberal reforms in the Papal States, he proved to be no friend of the

> *There have been wiser politicians and greater generals than Garibaldi; but none has been more lovable or more loved.*
> —JASPER RIDLEY
> historian

The Milan Cathedral. A five-day Milanese revolt marked the culmination of Italian dissatisfaction with Austrian rule and a turning point for the growth of revolutionary consciousness. However, Metternich's troops eventually crushed the insurrection in bloody street fighting.

Charles Albert, Piedmontese king of Sardinia and the father of Victor Emmanuel II. His surprising truce with the Austrian foes after the Battle of Custozza infuriated Garibaldi and prompted the rousing Castelletto Manifesto.

unification effort. The pope had refused to send troops to fight against the Austrians, and he began to withdraw some of the reforms he had introduced. The radicals felt especially betrayed when Pio Nono appointed a conservative politician, Count Pellegrino Luigi Eduardo Rossi, as his prime minister. Within a few weeks, Rossi was assassinated. The pope fled to the Kingdom of the Two Sicilies, and the people of Rome established a republic with Mazzini at its head.

Garibaldi, meanwhile, had not been idle. For several months he had been reorganizing his Red Shirts and seeking a new place to fight. He left for Rome as soon as he heard the Republic had been established, because he knew that the monarchies of Europe would not rest until the pope had been restored to rule.

How right he was. Spain, Naples, France, and Austria united their forces for a massive assault on the Roman revolutionaries. First to arrive were the French, who landed 10,000 troops on the coast of Italy, about 40 miles from Rome. At the time, Garibaldi and his legion — now 1,300 strong — were at Rieti, only a short distance away. Three days later he was in Rome.

Garibaldi immediately organized the defense of Rome. A key point was a hill outside the western wall of the city facing the French advance. On this hill stood a tall building, the Villa Corsini, and Garibaldi knew that if the French placed their cannons on it they could breach the wall and easily enter the city. Therefore, he made the Villa Corsini his headquarters and increased his forces to about 2,500 men. There he waited until the French arrived on the morning of April 30.

Not expecting a fight, the French were unprepared for the stiff resistance they encountered. At a critical moment Garibaldi ordered an assault on the French, who retreated in disorder. Garibaldi lost 200 men; the French lost almost 1,000 men, some 400 as prisoners to the elated revolutionaries. Although Garibaldi wanted to chase the French as they fled and give them a thorough drubbing, Mazzini and his advisers refused to allow it, thinking that a pacific gesture would induce their enemies to accept the Republic in Rome. It was to be a vain hope.

Although the French encouraged the idea of an armistice and retreated to their seaport base at Civitavecchia, they were actually biding their time until reinforcements could arrive. Meanwhile, other enemies of the Roman Republic challenged the revolutionaries. As Mazzini was signing a 15-day ceasefire with the French, Garibaldi and his legionnaires were confronting a Neapolitan army coming from the south. At the village of Velletri, Garibaldi met the Neapolitans in a brutal engagement that almost cost him his life. The Neapolitan cavalry had overwhelmed his own mounted troops, who began retreating in great disorder. Garibaldi, positioned slightly behind the line of battle, was watching the confrontation from horseback, and when he saw his troops begin to withdraw he rode forward to block their path and tried to rally them. With him went Aguiar, his Brazilian orderly.

It was a foolhardy thing to do, because the fleeing

Garibaldi received a hero's welcome at the Milan train station in 1848. Despite Charles Albert's rejection of his aid, he was appointed a general and assembled a small army with which he intended to wage his own war against the Austrians.

Mazzini's idealism often clashed with Garibaldi's more pragmatic views, cutting short their collaboration. Although generated by true revolutionary thinking, Mazzini's schemes were too vague or impractical to succeed.

cavalrymen could not stop their horses in time, and they crashed headlong into Garibaldi and Aguiar. In an instant the road was a tangle of fallen horses and men, and on the bottom of this heap were Garibaldi and Aguiar. They lay helpless as the Neapolitan cavalry jumped into the melee, slashing away with their sabers at the unhorsed legionnaires. A terrible slaughter was averted when a detachment of Garibaldi's infantry rushed forward and repelled the Neapolitans. Miraculously, neither Garibaldi nor Aguiar was seriously hurt.

Again, Garibaldi wanted to press his advantage and inflict a decisive defeat on his fleeing foes, and again his superiors ruled otherwise. They did not want to leave Rome defenseless while Garibaldi pursued the enemy; he, in turn, urged them to abandon Rome, because it was futile to attempt the city's defense with the small army available to the Republic. Events were to bear out Garibaldi's prediction.

With the 15-day armistice drawing to a close, Mazzini ordered Garibaldi back to Rome. There was no urgency, Mazzini believed, because the French official who negotiated the armistice assured him the fighting would not begin again until June 4. At the Villa Corsini, Garibaldi's headquarters and a key point in any defense of the city, the guards were asleep when French troops captured it on the evening of June 2.

Garibaldi was lying sick in bed when he heard the awful news. He rushed to the west wall and decided the Villa Corsini had to be recaptured at all costs. Of Rome's 18,000 soldiers, he commanded 6,000, and these he sent against the French. Unfortunately, not only did the French now have the advantage of terrain but also of numbers — 20,000 to Garibaldi's 6,000.

A monumental arch honoring the Italians who died attempting to recapture the Villa Corsini now stands on the spot. The Corsini straddled a sloping hill behind a low wall topped with a row of potted plants. It made a perfect hiding place for sharpshooters. To make matters worse for an attacking force, there were two lanes up to the villa, each bordered by high hedges. The lanes met at the gate to the villa, its only entrance. Italian historians call this spot the Death Angle, because attacking troops had to squeeze through the gate, where they were easy targets for the French cannoneers and riflemen.

For an entire day the French and Italians fought for that piece of ground. The Italians would capture it, only to be driven back by French counterattacks, and then the deadly exchange would begin again. Whatever can be said about Garibaldi — and historians have criticized his strategy that terrible day — he was no coward. As cheering revolutionaries rushed toward the Death Angle, the general sat calmly on his white horse, watching the battle, clearly exposed to enemy fire. Although bullets continually grazed his poncho, to the astonishment of onlookers, he remained unhurt. He sent wave after wave of brave Italians against the French. But it

All Europe watched as Spain, Naples, France, and Austria launched a massed assault on the revolutionaries in Rome, where a people's republic had been established. This cover from an 1849 English weekly magazine showed the entrance to Garibaldi's headquarters.

would have taken more than bravery to dislodge the French from their strong position. At the end of the day, after 17 hours of continuous fighting, after losing more than 200 of his own legionnaires and more than 1,000 men altogether, Garibaldi admitted defeat.

Rome was doomed, but it took a month before its defense totally collapsed. "No surrender!" was the cry as men and women fought the French wall by wall, street by street. Hundreds of patriots died during the tragic siege, among them scores of boys and girls, some as young as 12 years of age, who fought alongside the adults. In a typical show of fanaticism three Italian officers charged to their deaths, each smoking a cigar and swinging a saber; with them died a young girl armed only with a bayonet.

Mazzini, to whom Rome was sacred ground, at one point wanted to employ the strategy of simply sending massed crowds of men, women, and children against the attackers and hoping there would be more survivors than bullets in the French guns, thereby achieving victory over the bodies of heroic but suicidal patriots. Once again Garibaldi and Mazzini quarreled. This was no way to fight a war, Garibaldi argued, and fortunately the idea was abandoned.

Garibaldi had long disagreed with Mazzini on political and military questions. He had disagreed with the republican leader on the issue of dictatorship: to Garibaldi it was the only way to solidify resistance against the enemy. Strategically, the defense of Rome seemed not nearly as important as setting up a guerrilla campaign in the nearby hills and mountains. Although Garibaldi did as Mazzini implored him to do (with disastrous results), tensions between the two patriots had undermined their ability to understand one another.

Although the fall of Rome seemed imminent, the revolutionaries did not lose heart. Morale, in fact, remained high. The leaders of the republican government, including Garibaldi, signed an appeal to the people on June 24 that declared: "Behind the first bulwark the enemy will find a second wall, and behind that the barricades of the people." As another morale booster, Garibaldi issued red shirts to all the men in his legion, which now numbered less than 1,000. Until then only the men who had come with him from Montevideo had actually worn the distinctive garb of the *Garibaldini*, or Garibaldians, the patriot's armed followers. Sadly, many of the red-clad recruits were killed within a few days.

Shortly after Garibaldi issued his appeal, Anita arrived in Rome. Although pregnant with their fifth child, and despite her husband's stern warnings to remain in Nice, Anita felt Garibaldi needed her at this dark moment. Never one to shrink from danger, she managed to sneak into the besieged city.

On June 30 the French mounted their final attack. The fighting was intense, as both sides sensed

Garibaldi leads his Red Shirts in a charge against French troops at the Villa Corsini. The newly appointed general was often depicted in the popular press as fearless and all but indestructible.

Four thousand men voluntarily mustered outside St. Peter's Basilica on the evening before Rome ceded to the French in defeat. Garibaldi exhorted them: "Those of you who love your country and love glory, follow me!"

the end approaching. As one French assault was repulsed, another was launched. Even Garibaldi was in the front lines, slashing at the enemy with his cavalry saber. Unfortunately, valor alone could not stop the French. By the end of the day they controlled most of the key positions, and many of Garibaldi's Red Shirts, including the ever-faithful Aguiar, were dead.

That night, as the French regrouped for renewed fighting in the morning. Garibaldi, meanwhile, was called away to the capital. He left his men and decided to take his proposals personally to the Constituent Assembly in Turin, which was then debating what was to be done. The assembly fell silent as the weary warrior entered the chamber. His face was flecked with dirt and gore, his red shirt was stiff from the dried blood of the enemies who had fallen by his hand, and his sword was so battered he could push it only partway into his scabbard. The members of the assembly cheered as he walked stiffly to the platform.

The assembly was debating three options: to surrender, to fight to the death, or — Garibaldi's reasoned suggestion — to evacuate Rome. "We are the Republic," he reminded the politicians; the government could be set up somewhere else. The frightened deputies did not want to take this step. Indeed, most of them wanted to surrender. Time was needed before an agreement could be reached, so they requested a temporary armistice from the French.

On July 2 the assembly decided to end the resistance. The deputies called on Garibaldi to meet with them and made him general in chief of the Republican army, thereby giving him permission to withdraw from Rome with as many men as were willing to follow him.

Four thousand volunteered. They assembled that evening in the Great Square of St. Peter's Basilica — a few survivors from Montevideo, students, soldiers. Most were on foot; a few were on horseback, including Garibaldi and Anita, who refused to remain behind. Dressed in men's clothes, with her hair cut short, she joined Garibaldi as he took the first steps on his path of no return.

Watching this dramatic moment were thousands of Romans, many of them wives, relatives, and friends of those about to leave. Many were weeping, pleading with their loved ones not to go. When Garibaldi and Anita appeared, the crowd cheered wildly. Moving his dignified white horse into the center of the throng and asking for silence, he made a simple but eloquent speech. "Fortune, who betrays us today, will smile on us tomorrow. I am going out from Rome. This is what I have to offer to those who wish to follow me: hunger, cold, the heat of the sun; no wages, no barracks, no ammunition, but continual skirmishes, forced marches and bayonet-fights. Those of you who love your country and love glory, follow me!"

Garibaldi and his little legion left Rome on July 3. The French entered the city 21 hours later.

'Long live the Republic' is the cry with which people endure the pain of amputation and even death itself. One hour of life in Rome is worth a century of normal existence.
—GIUSEPPE GARIBALDI
from a June 1849
letter to his wife

5

Retreat to Fight Again

When Garibaldi retreated from Rome, he expected to continue the fight against the French by raising a large army from the citizenry outside Rome. This hope was quickly dashed. He not only failed to get more recruits but also had difficulty obtaining food for his men, as four enemy armies — from Spain, France, Austria, and Naples, 80,000 strong—began a relentless pursuit.

In trying to escape, Garibaldi faced several problems. First, he had only paper money issued by the Republic of Rome with which to pay for food and ammunition. As soon as the French captured the city this currency became worthless. Second, the farther from Rome, the less fervent was republican sentiment among the people. Finally, the armies pursuing Garibaldi called him an outlaw and threatened to execute anyone giving him or his followers any assistance. This was no idle threat. The Austrians had given ample proof of their cruelty, going so far as to execute several captured stragglers, including a group of young boys no older than 12 or 13. Within a few days the situation of the retreating republicans had become desperate, and Garibaldi's men began to desert, a few at a time at first and then in increasing numbers.

Garibaldi quickly abandoned his plan to continue the revolution and now sought only to get his band to safety. First he went south as though he were

The failed revolution of 1848 once more rendered Garibaldi an exile and ordinary citizen. Within a decade, he reemerged from his island home of Caprera to renew his role as a man of destiny.

Gasperone, at top, had been hired by the Bourbons to assassinate Garibaldi. The hired killer became so impressed with the general while pursuing him that he ultimately joined the Red Shirts.

heading for Naples. He doubled back and then marched west toward the coast before heading north toward Venice, where revolutionaries were still at war with Austria. It is a credit to his leadership that he was able to avoid a fight with his pursuers for more than three weeks. His army could move only as fast as his slowest foot soldiers, and most of his men were on foot. Altogether he had about 100 cavalrymen, who acted as his scouts and spies. Half protected the head of the column; the rest covered the flanks and rear. In addition, Garibaldi had a few wagons to carry supplies and one small cannon.

After almost four weeks of insufficient food, sleepless nights, and searing heat, with his army melting away before his eyes, Garibaldi decided to abandon his attempt to reach Venice and sought asylum in San Marino instead. This little republic, an independent state for 900 years, was no more than 12 miles long and 4 miles wide, but to Garibaldi it seemed to be his last hope. Reaching there on the morning of July 30, his army now reduced to 1,800 men, he asked for asylum and was refused. Garibaldi waited a day and then tried again, promising to surrender all his arms. Although the San Marino officials agreed, it was too late. While Garibaldi was away an Austrian army attacked his men and scattered them in every direction. Anita, heroic as ever, had tried to organize a resistance but failed. Only the cannoneers, who had dragged their little gun all the way from Rome, had stood their ground. But eventually even they had to abandon it to the enemy and flee. When Garibaldi returned, he shepherded his remaining contingent into the temporary sanctuary of San Marino. The government of San Marino tried to arrange an honorable truce for Garibaldi with the Austrians at their border but to no avail. The Austrians wanted Garibaldi and his men punished for their "crimes."

Garibaldi decided to leave and try once more to reach Venice. Of his followers still with him, only 200 agreed to leave the safety of San Marino and hazard the dangerous journey. Among those he thought best to leave behind was Anita. She was now six months pregnant; over a few days' time, she had also become quite ill with a high fever. She was obviously in no condition for the attempted escape, but Garibaldi felt he had no choice but to take her with him.

Garibaldi left San Marino at midnight on the evening of July 31 by slipping out through one of the town gates. His plan was to sneak across the mountains to the Adriatic coast and then requisition as many fishing boats as were necessary to carry his men to Venice. Reaching the town of Cesenatico on the following night, Garibaldi commandeered 13 fishing boats and headed out to sea, leaving behind

> . . . not infrequently at the most difficult moments of my stormy life — as when I escaped unharmed from the waves of the ocean, or from the leaden hail of the battlefield — I seemed to see my loving mother bending and kneeling before the Infinite, a suppliant for the life of the child of her womb.
> —GIUSEPPE GARIBALDI

A newspaper sketch of the men with Garibaldi in Rome. After almost a month of grueling hardship in retreat, the weary general decided to seek asylum for his diminishing army in the tiny, independent republic of San Marino.

the white horse that had seen him safely through the siege of Rome and his incredible retreat. He gave it to a republican sympathizer with instructions to shoot it if it fell into Austrian hands.

At first it appeared that Garibaldi and his men were going to get away, but they were spotted by an Austrian naval patrol within 50 miles of Venice. Garibaldi blamed the moon, which was almost full that night. Whatever the astronomical conditions, the Austrians captured all but three of the boats, which carried about 30 Garibaldini, including the general and his wife. When these reached a nearby shore, Garibaldi told them to split up and escape as best they could. He did not realize that he had landed on an island.

As his followers disappeared into the night, Garibaldi was now alone except for Anita and one companion, Giovanni Culiolo, nicknamed "Leggero" because he had been limping since the siege of Rome from a bullet wound in his leg. This man, in fact, had been left behind when Garibaldi left Rome, but he had eventually caught up with his beloved leader and loyally remained. As for Anita, she was now so sick she could no longer walk and soon lapsed into delirium.

Garibaldi's situation seemed hopeless. He was on an island, surrounded by enemies, and his only companions were his helpless wife and a lame soldier. Then fate intervened, the sort of intervention that convinced the people of Italy that Garibaldi was a man of destiny.

As he and Anita lay hidden in a cornfield, Leggero scouted the area and returned with a man named Giacomo Bonnet, whom Garibaldi immediately recognized as a member of his Roman legion. Bonnet's brother, in fact, had died at Villa Corsini. Instead of joining Garibaldi's retreat Bonnet had gone home. Hearing the gunfire off the coast, he had gone to the beach and seen Garibaldi splash ashore. Now he was ready to help him escape.

Bonnet's appearance at this time must have seemed like a miracle to this desperate trio. He hid the three fugitives in a hut, got them fresh clothes, and then brought them to a farm while he arranged for a boat to take them off the island. Although he tried to persuade Anita to stay and see a doctor, she insisted on going with Garibaldi. Unfortunately, the boatman taking them to the mainland recognized Garibaldi and abandoned them on another island, claiming he would be killed by the Austrians for aiding and abetting the fugitives. There Garibaldi, Leggero, and Anita remained, shivering with cold and certain they were to be captured, after all.

Again fate intervened. Bonnet learned of the boatman's treachery and sent another boat to rescue Garibaldi. This boatman was a staunch republican and nationalist. He not only took them to shore but also arranged for a cart to carry Anita to a nearby farm. Although a doctor was summoned immediately, Anita was beyond help; she died within a few hours. Garibaldi could not even wait to see her buried. He and Leggero were rushed to another farm. Eventually, thanks to the republican underground, they were able to get across the mountains to Chiavari, near Genoa in the Kingdom of Sardinia, where, for a time at least, they were safe.

Fate was not so kind to their companions. Most

Whatever he did was done with passionate conviction and boundless enthusiasm, and a career full of color and incident makes him now seem one of the most romantic products of his age.
—DENIS MACK SMITH
British historian, on Garibaldi

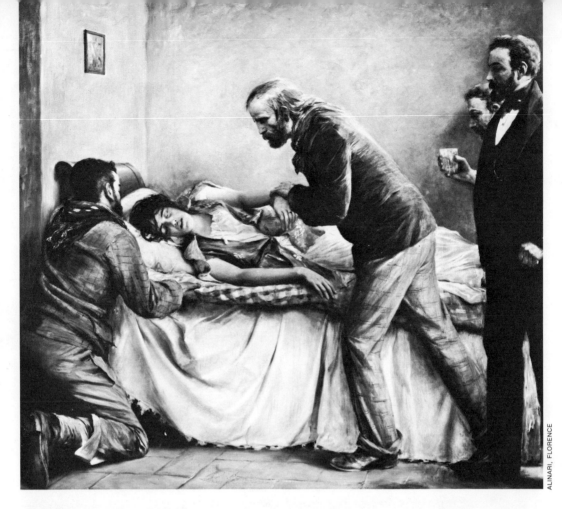

The death of Anita Garibaldi. Six months pregnant and ill with fever, she had refused to stay safely in San Marino when her husband attempted a dangerous escape. Garibaldi could not even wait to see her buried.

of the 30 Garibaldini who reached shore with them were captured. Of these, at least 10 were executed, including a 13-year-old boy, an officer who had been with Garibaldi in Montevideo, and a priest named Ugo Bassi. The authorities eventually arrested Bonnet, but he was released because they could not prove he had helped Garibaldi. The government of Italy later rewarded Bonnet with a pension for life.

Garibaldi's arrival in Piedmont caused a diplomatic dilemma. During the siege of Rome King Charles Albert had renewed his war with the Austrians, only to be soundly defeated at the Battle of Novara. As a result, he abdicated his throne in favor of his son, Victor Emmanuel II. The new king proved to be a good ruler and eventually became Garibaldi's staunchest ally, but now he had to be careful not to frighten the Austrians by appearing too friendly to the defeated revolutionary. Accordingly, Garibaldi was allowed a brief visit with his mother and children at Nice. Shortly afterward he was sent once again into exile even though several Piedmontese leaders wished they could do more for him. "Garibaldi is no ordinary man," one of them wrote. "It was a great mistake not to make use of him [in 1848]. If there is another war, he will be a man to employ. How he managed to save himself on this last occasion is really a miracle."

Another war seemed the farthest thing from Garibaldi's mind at this time, however. Anita's death and the failure of the Italian people to rally behind him had depressed him greatly. Now, he said, he only wanted to live in the United States and start a new life for himself.

He eventually got to the United States, but it was no simple matter. In September 1849 Garibaldi left Italy with Leggero and another Red Shirt named Cucelli, who had been the musician of the Italian Legion; he stopped briefly in Tunis, Gibraltar, and Tangier before finally embarking for the United States in June 1850. Although he left Leggero and Cucelli in Tangier because he could not afford to pay their passage, he did have one companion, another legionnaire named Major Bovi. This officer had lost his right arm in the defense of Rome, and Garibaldi thought he would have difficulty making a living with such a handicap.

Upon arriving in New York, Garibaldi became the toast of the city. Crowds besieged him everywhere, and newspaper reporters gave him no rest. The people of the United States would have made a bigger fuss over this gentle, humble leader, but he refused to allow it. As he wrote in a letter published in the New York press: "Though a public manifestation of this feeling might yield much gratification to me, an exile from my native land, severed from my children, and mourning the overthrow of my country's freedom by means of foreign interference, yet believe me that I would rather . . . be permitted, quietly and humbly, to become an American citizen of this great Republic of Freemen . . . and await a more favorable opportunity for the redemption of my country from foreign and domestic oppressors."

Victor Emmanuel II became king of Sardinia when Charles Albert abdicated the throne after a decisive defeat at Novara. He became Garibaldi's staunchest ally and a leading proponent of Italian unification.

The rock of Gibraltar, between Spain and North Africa. Garibaldi set out for the United States after again being exiled. He first spent time in Tunis, Gibraltar, and Tangier, where he began his autobiography.

And this is exactly what he did. For a time he lived on Staten Island with an Italian candle maker named Meucci, working as his helper. Although seriously hampered by rheumatism, Garibaldi toiled as an unskilled laborer. His job was to carry barrels of tallow from the wharf to Meucci's factory.

Meanwhile, Italian revolutionaries in other parts of the world were not content to let their illustrious leader slip into obscurity. They bought a ship in San Francisco, sailed it to Callao, and arranged for Garibaldi to come to Peru to take command. He was captain of this vessel for one year, and then captain of another, which he sailed to London in February

1854. There he met several times with Mazzini, who had remained an adamant revolutionary. The problem was that his schemes—though visionary—were too vague and impractical to succeed. Garibaldi also met other prominent figures involved with the revolutionary movements of the day, such as the Russian Aleksandr Herzen. Herzen is credited with founding populism, a political doctrine resting on the notion that proposals for reform should be brought directly to the common people and peasantry. In Russia, Herzen believed that the peasants would provide the basis for the revolution, since it was for their welfare and freedom that oppressive rulers would be overthrown. After meeting Garibaldi in London, Herzen noted that the freedom fighter was severely critical of Mazzini, saying that he was out of touch with the Italian people. After this visit, Garibaldi did not return to the United States. In-

A memorial to Garibaldi on Staten Island, New York. He lived quietly there for two years and worked for an Italian candlemaker until he set sail for Peru and, eventually, England.

stead, in April he went to Genoa to see his children, visited the grave of his mother, who had died while he was away, and then purchased some land on the island of Caprera, a rather desolate spot just off the northeast tip of Sardinia.

By 1856 there was a plot afoot to rescue some political prisoners held by the king of Naples at San Stefano. With British assistance, which included providing a ship, Garibaldi was to head the operation, but the vessel later sank and the plan came to nothing. He remained for five years at Caprera. During that time he built a cottage with the help of his 15-year-old son Menotti and, for all intents and purposes, seemed prepared to live out his life in quiet retirement.

Anita may very likely have been his one true love, but he seldom wanted for female companionship, and he sired a number of children by several women, none of them highborn. His romantic affairs were not restricted to women of any one class. While in London, his reputation as a swashbuckler and gallant warrior had won him many admirers — especially among women of society. Garibaldi was physically attractive but also possessed an intangible personal magnetism, what one acquaintance called an "irresistible spell." In London he was the embodiment of the populist myth of the noble, pure, and simple peasant who represented the struggle for liberty and self-determination.

Garibaldi regarded the quiet interlude in his life from 1854 to 1859 as being of little significance. It was a time of frequent travels abroad and various business ventures. But it was also in 1854 that he became engaged to Emma Roberts, a widow who had inherited substantial wealth. The pair remained engaged until 1856, and he subsequently named a 40-ton boat after his fiancée. He sailed about Italy on this vessel until its ultimate destruction in 1857.

That same year the socialite Baroness Maria Espérance von Schwartz visited him at his rugged island home. She was a writer of romances and wanted to publicize Garibaldi's life. One of her projects had been to gain funding for a monument to commemorate Garibaldi's late wife, Anita.

Scenes from Garibaldi's rustic life on Caprera. He was known to admire Robinson Crusoe and built a house and barns with only his son's aid. For five years he remained relatively isolated from politics and history.

The brilliant Count di Cavour was prime minister and premier as the effort for Italian unification intensified. His Plombières agreement gambled on a temporary alliance with France against Austria and on Garibaldi's willingness to lead Italy's war.

He had other female admirers, such as the countess Maria Martini della Torre, who literally went mad over Garibaldi after volunteering to join his Red Shirts. From his days in London he also captivated the duchess of Sutherland, whose letters to the Italian patriot were explicitly passionate.

Finally, in June 1859 he met the 17-year-old Marchesina Giuseppina Raimondi and married her in 1860. She was the illegitimate daughter of a nobleman, who was relieved to have her married off to the hero; meanwhile, even Victor Emmanuel cruelly mocked the 52-year-old Garibaldi's scandalous infatuation.

Again fate took matters into its own hands. As Garibaldi farmed the sparse, stony soil and tended his sheep and goats, the spirit of revolution again swept the Italian peninsula. The Risorgimento was revived with even greater vigor than before, and as the Piedmontese official had predicted 10 years earlier, if there was fighting to do, Garibaldi was the man to do it.

This time Mazzini was not at the helm of the unification movement. A brilliant statesman, Count Camillo Benso di Cavour, the prime minister of the Kingdom of Sardinia since 1852, had emerged with his own plan for gaining Italian self-determination. Unlike the idealistic Mazzini, Cavour was no visionary but a skilled politician and diplomat. Furthermore, Cavour disliked Mazzini and did not support a revolutionary solution. Mazzini was a romantic who harbored dreams of a European community in which no single nation would dominate any other; such ideas eventually caused Garibaldi, a simple man of action, to drift away from his former mentor. As for Cavour, an intellectual like Mazzini, he had gained great wealth through business dealings. However, his unemotional and extremely practical outlook did not make him many friends within Sardinia's political establishment. He also had no illusions concerning Italian "liberty" as prophesied by Mazzini, who declared, "Without liberty there is no true morality."

In his youth, Cavour had drawn much of his original inspiration to lead the Italian unification movement from the Paris revolution of 1830. But his early revolutionary ardor quickly hardened into more rational political methods, relying primarily on diplomacy and compromise. Having observed the progress made in England against economic hardship and injustice through the enactment of new laws, Cavour firmly supported gradual reforms. Cavour's ultimate aim, like that of Mazzini and Garibaldi, was still to win independence for all Italian states. Contrary to Garibaldi's unalloyed optimism, however, Cavour was not so certain that Austria was "a colossus of clay crumbling to bits." Moreover, for Cavour, the most significant issue remained how to free Italy from foreign domination and at the same time foil the desire of radicals who wanted to do away with the power of the king and the pope. Garibaldi advocated a united Italy with the king as dictator, whereas Cavour was stolidly in favor of a constitutional monarchy — a king with limited powers. Cavour's loyalty was first to King Victor Emmanuel and then to the Italian people. Although relations between Cavour and the patriot Garibaldi would eventually break down completely, it was Cavour's own newspaper, *Il Risorgimento*, founded in 1847 and coedited by Luigi Farini, that furnished the unification movement with its famous name. It had also been Cavour who penned an article urging on the rebellions of 1848: "One way alone is open for the nation, the government, the King. War! Immediate war."

Cavour wanted to see Italy united, but united on his own terms under Victor Emmanuel as king of all Italy. To achieve this goal, Cavour realized, he needed Garibaldi. But first he had to engineer the right situation in which to use his services. In July 1858 at the spa of Plombières, Cavour succeeded in arranging an alliance against Austria with France, the nation that traditionally had every reason to oppose and stamp out an Italian independence movement.

Cavour was confident that he could look to France and England for "some remedy to the ills of Italy," especially since Sardinia had fought beside the two nations against the Russians in the Crimean War

THE BETTMANN ARCHIVE/BBC HULTON

A daguerrotype of Garibaldi, who abandoned his peaceful life on Caprera in 1859. He was willing to ally himself with royalists for the sake of Italy in spite of suspicions he held about the wily Cavour.

(1854–56). Emperor Napoleon III of France had no illusions, however, about helping the Italians. He simply saw an opportunity to push his Austrian rivals from the Italian peninsula.

Under the Plombières agreement, Italy would be divided into four states headed by the pope, who would serve as president of the resulting new confederation. Napoleon expected the pope's cooperation in this plan, because it was the French who protected his political authority in Italy. Renamed "Upper Italy," Sardinia would then absorb Lombardy, Venetia, Parma, Modena, and much of the Papal States, while ceding to France the provinces of Nice and Savoy. Rome would be the pope's sole jurisdiction. The Kingdom of Naples would retain its current status. Finally, an arranged marriage would establish an alliance between the Piedmontese house of Savoy and the French monarchy. Once married to Victor Emmanuel's daughter, Napoleon's nephew, Prince Napoleon Bonaparte ("Plon-Plon"), would rule over a new kingdom in central Italy. All this ultimately hinged on the actual outcome of the conflict with Austria.

Although Cavour was taking an enormous gamble, he was doing so to regain Italian lands, not to help the French emperor take over what the Austrians already controlled. According to Cavour's scheme, the Kingdom of Sardinia would recover the territories in question for Italy while the unwitting French supplied their cooperation and support. But Cavour was prepared to pacify the French, when necessary, by making small concessions along the way.

The Sardinian prime minister announced his intention to free Lombardy and Venetia from Austrian rule, thus provoking an attack by the Austrians. For Cavour's purposes, it was necessary that Austria appear to be the aggressor. At the same time, Cavour assured France that his objective was not to unite Italy as one country but merely to create a loose collection of states independent of Austria and under the "protection" of Sardinia and the pope.

The need for war against the Austrians caused Cavour to cast about for a general capable of liberating these territories from Austrian control. Garibaldi, of course, was the leader the prime minister needed once the war was in full swing. In their first meeting in August 1856 Cavour sensed that Garibaldi was not about to lead revolts for the republican cause, as were Mazzini and the other nationalist leader, Carlo Pisacane. These republicans wanted to establish a democratic state while fighting to free parts of Italy from Austrian domination. Garibaldi, now disenchanted with Mazzini, might be willing to ally himself with royalists — supporters of monarchy — like Cavour. Garibaldi was suspicious of Cavour's motives, however, thinking that the wily politician was trying to further the interests of Piedmont and not those of all Italy.

By the end of 1858, Cavour was ready to enlist Garibaldi's aid. Three times he sent for the "hermit of Caprera," as he called him, before Garibaldi finally came to Turin in March 1859.

One day Cavour's servant announced that a visitor who refused to give his name had arrived to see the prime minister. "He has a big stick and a big hat, and he says he has an appointment" was all the servant could report.

"Ah," said Cavour, "I have been expecting him. Bring him in."

> *Whereas Cavour applied a highly sophisticated intelligence to politics and prepared every political move with extreme care, Garibaldi believed in direct action; and he had the courage to take such action no matter how great the odds against him.*
> —NORMAN RICH
> American historian

6

The Thousand

Following his meeting with Cavour, Garibaldi agreed to resume his efforts for a united Italy, this time by allying himself with Victor Emmanuel and the Kingdom of Sardinia. Some of the diehard radicals (Mazzini among them) criticized the aging warrior for abandoning his republican principles, but Garibaldi paid them no heed. "Although a born revolutionary," he later wrote, ". . . I have not failed, when necessary, to submit myself to that necessary discipline which is indispensable to the good success of any enterprise." In this case, it meant trusting Cavour and Victor Emmanuel when they said they needed his help in bringing about a united Italy. "And as I was convinced . . . that Italy should march with Victor Emmanuel to free herself from foreign domination, I thought that I should subject myself to his orders at all cost, and silence my Republican conscience." By making this decision, Garibaldi went on to his finest moment as a revolutionary.

It was not an easy alliance, however. Although appointed a major general in the Sardinian army by Cavour, he was not given an official commission by Victor Emmanuel. Nor were his troops treated as part of the Sardinian armed forces. They were even trained separately from them. Their camp was 40 miles away from Turin, the capital of Piedmont. Although Garibaldi viewed these policies as a personal slight, Cavour was merely trying to appease his

How happy my mother should be for giving me life in this wonderful period of Italian history.
—GIUSEPPE GARIBALDI

A rare portrait of Garibaldi in a formal uniform, which he wore after he seized power from the Austrians in Naples in 1860. The former republican achieved his finest and most controversial moments by allying himself with King Victor Emmanuel.

French allies, who were somewhat suspicious of finding themselves working in concert with their former adversary. Thus, Cavour kept Garibaldi in the background as much as possible. Throughout the subsequent campaigns Garibaldi operated independently of the Sardinian army, fighting a guerrilla war. In this respect, little had changed since 1848.

Garibaldi and Cavour also disagreed on the ultimate goal to be attained. In typically dramatic terms, Garibaldi forcefully presented his view that all governing power should be handed over to Victor Emmanuel. "This will quiet the jealousy and bickering which is unfortunately a quality of us Italians." The king "knows what must be done," Garibaldi told Cavour. "Everyone is convinced that we need a military dictatorship; so, by God, let it be absolute; . . . *No trouble-makers at any cost.*" Given his belief that the king's powers should be limited by a constitution and that free elections were necessary, Cavour could not agree with this extreme demand. These differences, of course, could be reconciled once unity was achieved; for now, this reconciliation was as far away as ever. As for "trouble-makers," Cavour, along with the minister of war, General Alfonso La Marmora, believed volunteer militia organizations were a potential threat. The prime minister intended to keep an eye on Garibaldi and to control the number of men under his command.

Garibaldi did his part. Leading the *Cacciatori delle Alpi* (the Alpine Rifles), a force of about 3,000 men, he prowled the mountains of Lombardy, striking at Austrian units with the hit-and-run tactics he had learned in South America and perfected during subsequent fighting in Italy. Garibaldi was now a recognized and feared *partigiano*, or partisan.

The culmination of the war of 1859 was the Battle of Solferino (known in Italy as San Martino), in which the forces of Victor Emmanuel soundly defeated the Austrians, driving them out of Lombardy once and for all. Garibaldi had been recruited to lead this invasion — but only as second-in-command. This had not been to the patriot's liking from the outset. His was an imperious personality. Later to become prime minister, Francesco Crispi remarked that he had known no one with a greater strength of will than Garibaldi.

On May 24 Garibaldi won against Austrian troops in a conventional battle at Varese. He had not been discouraged by his obvious military disadvantages and, as usual, went on the attack. He managed to gain the upper hand even without cavalry or artillery. The Austrians tried taking the town back but failed, losing more than 100 men in the attempt. Garibaldi, emboldened after the Cacciatori had shown they were a match for the Austrians, attacked again at San Fermo. A short time later, he learned of the defeat inflicted on the Austrians by the combined forces of France and Sardinia at the Battle of Magenta on June 4, and also four days earlier at Palestro.

After losing at Magenta, the Austrians retreated and dug in on the bluffs near Solferino in Lombardy. But the French and 25,000 Sardinian troops had pursued them. The antagonists were roughly equal in numbers. Before these events began to take shape, Cavour had held talks with one of the future commanders at the impending Battle of Solferino — Emperor Napoleon III. During these talks, the em-

A panoramic painting shows Napoleon III, the French emperor and erratic ally of Italy, surveying the Battle of Solferino. At its conclusion Austrian forces had been driven from the Lombard province once and for all.

A woodcut of Garibaldi dated May 1859. His reputation and popularity remained intact despite his absence from Solferino. By the beginning of 1860, plans to engineer a united Italy were falling into place.

peror urged Cavour not to hinder the fighting, refused to sanction newly liberated territory as belonging to Sardinia, and ended by postponing the talks until a later date. British historian Patrick Turnbull sums up the tensions with which Cavour had to cope: "It exasperated him to think that Piedmont's liberty of action was still largely dependent on French bayonets."

Garibaldi, his forces bounding ahead of the regular armies of France and Sardinia, was suddenly ordered to head off Austrian advances in the Valtellino Valley. He and his sharpshooters found themselves removed from the most decisive battle of the war. It was during this uneventful maneuver that he also learned of the ensuing Treaty of Villafranca.

Solferino was a confrontation of the emperors: Emperor Franz Joseph of Austria, Napoleon III of France, and the Sardinian king, Victor Emmanuel, of the house of Savoy. All were on the field of battle.

One Italian general, Enrico Cialdini, who fought at Palestro and served with distinction in the Crimean War, would lead the 4th Division at Solferino. Cialdini was a bitter rival and critic of Garibaldi. Three years later, in 1862, an impatient Garibaldi went on an ill-fated offensive against Pope Pius IX's French defenders in order to capture Rome. It was to be Cialdini, under orders from the new king of Italy, who would rush to the scene to intercept Garibaldi's forces at Aspromonte. There Italian regulars apprehended Italian patriots.

At Solferino on June 24, Sardinian and French soldiers hurled themselves at the Austrian position and triumphed in what turned into a vicious melee in the torrid summer heat. Franz Joseph's armies were forced to abandon their stronghold after losing 20,000 men in fierce combat. The outcome was not all that Victor Emmanuel and Cavour had expected, for Napoleon was so appalled by the mayhem and bloodshed he had helped bring about that he at once decided to make peace with the Austrians. In a house formerly held by the Austrians the French emperor had set up his battle headquarters. On one of its walls an unknown Austrian had scrawled "*Addio cara Italia*" ("Good-bye, dear Italy"). But Napoleon was not proud of this accomplishment.

Cavour's strategy appeared to be working perfectly, but in his moment of triumph he received the startling news that the French had made a secret treaty with the Austrians at Villafranca on July 11. Napoleon had an abrupt change of heart. Perhaps he came to the realization that Cavour had a hidden agenda, that France would be next, once Austria was defeated. "I have the revolution at my tail," he told Franz Joseph I, the Austrian emperor. Whatever his reason, Napoleon's decision so angered Cavour that he resigned as prime minister of Sardinia.

THE BETTMANN ARCHIVE

The meeting of Franz Joseph of Austria and Napoleon III at Villafranca following Austria's defeat in Lombardy. The secret treaty between the two emperors enraged Cavour and threatened to upset Italy's hard-won advantage.

The situation was not entirely bleak, however. Lombardy was freed of Austrian control and became part of Sardinia, and Garibaldi had emerged with his reputation and popularity intact. Since there seemed to be no more fighting to do in the north, he took his best officers and moved south, to see about freeing the Papal States. He went on this mission having been led to think that he had carte blanche to invade the pope's dominion. He was pulled up short by none other than his king. He had barely reached central Italy when King Victor Emmanuel sent for him. The king urged the general to be patient. Why antagonize France at this time? he reasoned. As a Catholic country, it would naturally help the pope, as it had done in 1848. A better strategy would be to gain control of Naples and Sicily. Then the Papal States would be isolated and more easily absorbed into a united Italy.

Garibaldi's frustration was understandable. His expedition not only was abruptly canceled, but the leaders who had called on him expressly for the mission took the venture out from his command. Baron

Bettino Ricasoli, who had set up his own government in Florence in Tuscany, and Luigi Carlo Farini, dictatorial head of a rebel government in Modena, had appointed, instead, Sardinian general Manfredo Fanti to lead an army against the Papal States.

Patience was not one of Garibaldi's virtues, but he heeded his king, who gave him a splendid shotgun as a token of his appreciation. Following his audience with Victor Emmanuel, Garibaldi went to Genoa, taking with him about 1,000 members of the Cacciatori. There he remained for six months, waiting for the moment when he could return to the battlefield.

By the beginning of 1860, the time for waiting had ended. Victor Emmanuel had persuaded Cavour to return as prime minister, and the cunning politician pulled off a brilliant coup in March. Savoy and Nice were ceded to France. Thus Cavour made good his agreement with Napoleon, who was dissuaded from interfering in Sardinia's plans to engineer a united Italy.

Not surprisingly, Garibaldi was stunned when this news reached him. "Cavour has made me a foreigner!" he stormed. For the strong-willed patriot, such diplomatic trade-offs must have seemed incomprehensible. It was certainly ironic that a country already occupied by foreign governments would freely relinquish more of its own territory.

Only exciting developments in Sicily were able to distract Garibaldi from attempting to restore Nice to Italy. More than any part of Italy, Sicily was now inflamed with the spirit of rebellion and liberation. But the region's revolutionary sentiment was divided. There were those who wanted an alliance with Mazzini and his republicans; another camp saw salvation in supporting the king of Sardinia; a third faction sought complete independence for the island of Sicily. The time seemed ripe for Garibaldi to lead an expedition to liberate Sicily, and Mazzini urged him to do so. Garibaldi was reluctant. Mazzini's plans often failed. In any event, Garibaldi's loyalty was now to the crown and the house of Savoy, not the republicans.

> *At the side of the Gentleman King, all rivalry must disappear, all rancor must be dissipated. I have only one cry, which I repeat: To arms, all of you, all of you!*
> —GIUSEPPE GARIBALDI
> rallying his supporters
> around Victor Emmanuel

Meanwhile, with Garibaldi still uncertain of his next move, volunteers were pouring in from all over Italy in order to take part in the Sicilian expedition. Soon Garibaldi, whose own patriotic fervor knew no bounds, again began to wear the uniform of the Red Shirts. Each volunteer was issued this uniform on his arrival in Genoa. "Those who remember that day," wrote a historian who interviewed some of the volunteers in their old age, "speak of it as something too sacred ever to return. Italy has never seen the like of 1860 again."

Although he soon had 1,000 volunteers in his camp, Garibaldi was not yet convinced he should invade Sicily. He knew that the Neapolitan army there was more than 25,000 strong, and he feared a reprise of his experiences in 1848 when the country folk refused to help him during the disastrous retreat from Rome. Finally, patriotism and enthusiasm prevailed, and Garibaldi agreed to go.

On the evening of May 5, Garibaldi sailed from Genoa with 1,000 men on two ships, the *Piemonte* and the *Lombardo*, which his men had commandeered at gunpoint. For weapons they had obsolete muskets. Ammunition was in short supply. No matter. Garibaldi's volunteers — the Thousand, as they are known, the "Minute Men" of Italian history — considered themselves invincible and destined to succeed. They were soldiers in name only, however. Most were urban laborers. The rest were doctors, lawyers, engineers, artists, and businessmen. The Thousand ranged in age from 12 years to 60. All but 17 of them were Italians, and they were prepared to die for their country. Like the celebrated independence fighters the Cairoli brothers, many of them did. Of the five sons of this family who fought with Garibaldi in his various campaigns, four were killed. But the survivor, Benedetto, went on to become prime minister of a united Italy.

The invasion almost failed before it began. Garibaldi had chosen the Sicilian port of Marsala in which to disembark with his army. As they entered the harbor, two Neapolitan gunboats spotted them. Fortunately, Garibaldi was able to land his soldiers before the Neapolitans began counterattacking. What saved them from certain disaster were their

red shirts. The Neapolitan commander at first thought they were British soldiers and therefore delayed taking any action until it was too late.

Once safe on Sicilian soil, Garibaldi wasted no time before moving inland. When his forces reached the town of Salemi on May 12, Garibaldi declared himself the governor of Sicily while taking possession of the island in the name of Victor Emmanuel. His destination was Palermo, the capital, some 60 miles away. But between his Red Shirts and the capital was a Neapolitan army of 3,000 men, barring his path at Calatafimi. In their first great military test, the Red Shirts gloried in their victory. Garibaldi's triumph was especially important in convincing the people of Sicily to rally to his banner. Thus, as his Red Shirts passed through village after village on the way to Palermo, they were greeted by cheering crowds and offered gifts of food and supplies. Many of those who hailed the brightly clad liberators from the roadsides were ready to join Garibaldi's forces.

Although the support of the civilians was en-

Garibaldi and his men arrive in the Sicilian port of Marsala with the Neapolitans in close pursuit. The Red Shirts quickly moved inland to Salemi, where Garibaldi declared himself governor of Sicily.

couraging, Garibaldi knew that his most difficult chores still lay ahead. Palermo, a beautiful Mediterranean seaport on the northern coast of Sicily, contained a garrison of more than 20,000 Neapolitan troops under Bourbon command. Capturing it was bound to be a test of his men's valor, for the enemy was no longer about to be caught by surprise. This time, to succeed, he needed the help of a popular uprising within the city. Rather than assault the city from the obvious direction, in a direct line from Calatafimi, Garibaldi decided to attack from the southeast instead of the southwest. This meant crossing extremely treacherous mountain terrain. To further deceive the vigilant enemy, he sneaked out of camp during the middle of the night. His volunteers' campfires were meant to continue burning brightly. He also sent 200 men in still another direction, hoping to convince the Neapolitans that

Garibaldi departs Genoa with the Thousand on May 5, 1860. The Thousand were soldiers in name only; most were volunteers with little or no fighting experience who were now en route to confront overwhelming odds.

he was retreating into the center of Sicily. After 10 days of playing cat and mouse, Garibaldi was prepared to attack Palermo. Instead of 1,000 men, he had approximately 750, but he had been assured by Sicilian partisans that once he got into the city, the people were prepared to help him.

Ready to defend the city for the Bourbon king of Naples was an army of 20,000. During the night of May 26, Garibaldi's men descended from the surrounding mountains for his planned assault on the capital. Garibaldi hoped he had found the weak link in the enemy's defenses. The spot he selected for his attack was a lightly guarded gate on the southeast side of the city. To reach it, however, Garibaldi's soldiers first had to cross two bridges.

Since the local partisans had requested the honor

Children of the Sicilian capital of Palermo were among those who fervently greeted Garibaldi and his thousand Red Shirts after the victory at Calatafimi. The strategy for taking Palermo relied on coordinating a popular uprising.

of leading the attack, Garibaldi, against his better judgment, gave them his permission. This ill-considered decision nearly resulted in disaster, for the zealous but untrained Sicilians broke and ran when the guards at the first bridge opened fire.

This was no time for second-guessing. "Charge!" Garibaldi shouted. "Forward into the center of the city!" With that he spurred his horse, and his men, with bayonets held high, cleared both bridges and burst through the gate. Once inside Palermo, they still had to run a mile-long gauntlet of suburban roads. Surviving this, they came upon a high barricade of stones and rubble with which the Neapolitans had blocked the street. Here the Red Shirts lost some of their finest officers as the men tore a

The Battle of Palermo raged for ten days, as rebellious citizens joined forces with Garibaldi's men to seize control of the city from 20,000 Neapolitan troops. The rebels achieved a stunning upset through their audacity, bravery, and good fortune.

path through the barricade with their bare hands. When the space was large enough Garibaldi, still on his horse, jumped through, still shouting, "To the center of the city!" He did not stop until he got to the market square, and there he was surrounded by thousands of frenzied people. It was 4:00 A.M.

Garibaldi now had his revolution, and he was demonstrating that he was the powerful *duce* (leader) the Sicilians had hoped for. Splitting his Red Shirts into small squads, he sent them into various sectors of the city to organize a defense among the rebelling citizens, who began erecting barricades at every strategic intersection. For weapons, most of the people had only knives, pitchforks, and homemade pikes, but they made effective use of these crude arms.

After 10 days of fierce combat the Bourbon commander requested a truce, and the city was in Garibaldi's hands. The moment could not have been more opportune: more than half of Garibaldi's men were wounded, and he was almost out of ammunition. Had the Neapolitans realized this, there would have been no truce, but Garibaldi managed to bluff them into concessions that enabled him to hold the city until reinforcements arrived. The truce was extended until June 6, when the Neapolitans capitulated and began evacuating the island of Sicily. Most of Sicily was under the insurgents' control by July, and in September the city of Naples fell to Garibaldi's volunteers. Once again, thanks to sheer audacity, bravery, and a kindly providence, Garibaldi had achieved a stunning victory.

The city of Salerno in the Kingdom of Naples (the mainland of the Kingdom of the Two Sicilies) was but another step in Garibaldi's remarkable road to total victory. During the next six months, he achieved one conquest after another. In the Battle of Milazzo on July 20, with reinforcements from Sardinia, he defeated the last 4,000 Bourbon troops remaining in Sicily. Eight hundred Garibaldini fell in battle, but the struggle had taken a much greater toll on the Bourbon troops, whose casualties numbered 24,000. Ultimately, the Bourbon army's fight-

He professed to be a radical republican and a believer in the freedom of the individual, but like many men of action he was willing to employ dictatorial methods to achieve his ends.
—NORMAN RICH
American historian,
on Garibaldi

Neapolitan troops surrender to Garibaldi (center) in southern Italy. Every town and village in the region was liberated during his men's dramatic march up the peninsula; the Bourbons' fighting ability had been shattered.

ing ability had been shattered. From there Garibaldi crossed the Straits of Messina onto the mainland and began a dramatic march up the peninsula, sweeping the Bourbon forces out of southern Italy and liberating every town and village along the way. With every step his army grew as volunteers flocked to his banner, still the red, green, and white tricolor of the Kingdom of Sardinia. With every step, the forces of the Kingdom of the Two Sicilies became more discouraged. One example of the sort of paralysis that gripped his foes is an incident that occurred when seven of the Garibaldini, lost on the wrong road near Calabria (the southernmost peninsula of the Italian mainland), encountered a battalion of Neapolitan troops and told them they were scouts for a large army just a short distance off. The Neapolitans immediately surrendered, dropped their guns, and went home. Finally, on September 5, 1860, even the king of Naples lost heart. Taking his family, he left the city, never to return. Two days later, Garibaldi moved into the palace and proclaimed himself dictator of Naples and Sicily. This action was perhaps Garibaldi's most controversial. What was behind Garibaldi's establishing a personal dictatorship? British historian Denis Mack Smith explains that Garibaldi apparently believed that as large a number of people as possible should be free to live as they chose: ". . . if he turned naturally to dictatorship, this was so that he might fight tyranny the more effectively and . . . force people to be free."

The old warrior's work was still incomplete, however. Although the king of Naples had withdrawn, he entertained hopes of recovering his throne, and he organized the remaining Bourbon forces along the Volturno River outside the city. Further complicating matters for Garibaldi was Cavour, who simply could not believe that his general did not

Garibaldi's triumphant entry into the Bourbon stronghold of Naples. When the Bourbon king fled, Garibaldi declared himself dictator of Naples and Sicily — by far the most controversial act of his career.

The matchless persona of Garibaldi provided a vital link between northern and southern Italy during the crucial push toward nationhood. Cavour doubted the general's motives, but King Victor Emmanuel maintained faith in his patriotism.

have his sights on becoming ruler of Italy. No one, Cavour believed, could be so selfless and sincere. Thus, instead of working energetically on Garibaldi's behalf, he often worked secretly against him. Garibaldi was as much aware as Cavour, however, of the difficulty in trying to control southern Italy from faraway Turin, the Sardinian capital. Garibaldi was an important link between north and south. It was vital that his leadership and influence be a force for bringing the two halves of Italy together and not to split them apart at this crucial moment.

Victor Emmanuel, however, trusted Garibaldi, and he proceeded to do his share to complete the unification of Italy. Personally taking the field at the head of the Sardinian army, Victor Emmanuel began moving south to link up with Garibaldi, fighting and defeating the armies of the Papal States as he went. By the end of September he was on the verge of entering the Kingdom of the Two Sicilies just as Garibaldi was preparing to fight the forces remaining loyal to the Bourbon king in the famous Battle of the Volturno.

It was Garibaldi's only experience in what is considered classic set-piece warfare. Opposing the Bourbon army of 50,000 men, he had less than half that number. His forces consisted of the last remnants of the Thousand—reinforcements sent to him by his republican allies and volunteers who had joined his banner during his triumphal march from Sicily. Many of these men were of dubious military ability. One critic thought they were more interested in impressing the women of Naples with their red shirts than in doing any real fighting.

Refusing to heed detractors, Garibaldi went on to lead these troops to a brilliant victory in the battle that raged for the first two days of October. Although casualties for each side were equal — some 2,000 killed, wounded, or missing — it was Garibaldi's leadership and boldness that carried the day.

Guerrilla, partisan, general, hero, Garibaldi was now the undisputed ruler of southern Italy. The moment of truth had arrived. Would he turn his back on supporters of democratic government and pop-

ular sovereignty around the world to become dictator of Italy? Or would he entrust his conquests to his king, as he had promised?

The answer came in a dramatic moment at dawn on the morning of October 26, 1860, when the armies of King Victor Emmanuel and Garibaldi met at a crossroads about 30 miles from Naples. Garibaldi and the king rode out to meet each other between their watchful armies. As they drew nearer, Garibaldi took off his hat. "I salute the first king of Italy," he said in a soft voice.

"How are you, dear Garibaldi," the king replied.

"Well, Your Majesty, and you?"

"Excellent," said the king with a smile. There was a prolonged pause as the king and the soldier shook hands. Then, side by side, they rode off, with soldiers of the Royal Army and Red Shirts riding two abreast, forming an escort.

An historic meeting of Victor Emmanuel and Garibaldi took place at a crossroads near Naples. As he had promised, Garibaldi consigned his conquests in southern Italy to his king, proving his devotion to the ideals of unification.

93

7

Father of United Italy

Garibaldi's hour of triumph was bittersweet at best. King Victor Emmanuel, although profoundly grateful to Garibaldi for his integral role in overcoming foreign domination, told him that his services were no longer needed and that the army of Piedmont would take over conduct of future military operations.

Garibaldi accepted this decision with characteristic grace and humility. When the king formally accepted control of Naples and Sicily, Garibaldi was in the throne room, and with the transfer of power he became an ordinary citizen once again. He was not curtly dismissed, however. The king offered to repay him with a castle, a title, and a pension for life. His extraordinary sense of honor and duty allowed him no alternative but to decline these awards. Accompanied by his son Menotti, who had fought with him as a member of the Thousand, Garibaldi returned to his little farm on Caprera.

But Garibaldi was not one to live out his years in quiet retirement. Whenever Cavour appeared to him to be straying from the course the old soldier thought proper for the Risorgimento, Garibaldi was loudly critical. He was especially disgruntled with the shabby treatment the Kingdom of Sardinia ac-

His ability to inspire affection, even idolatry, and his fearless, untiring labors for the national cause made him in time a patriotic legend.
—ARTHUR J. MAY
American historian,
on Garibaldi

The cause of nationalism remained the focal issue of Garibaldi's later life despite the king's decision to remove him from official military command. The 53-year-old hero continued to affect Italy's political course from Caprera.

Garibaldi rejected King Victor Emmanuel's offer of a castle, a title, and a pension, choosing instead to return to Caprera. He soon found himself caught up again in the struggle for Italian unity, which was to bring him into repeated contact with Victor Emmanuel throughout his later years.

corded the men who had fought for him. As volunteers they did not qualify for veterans' benefits as regularly enlisted soldiers did.

In addition to his continued interest in politics, Garibaldi had an adoring public to occupy his time. Journalists, romantics, and other admirers continually came to visit him at Caprera. In fact, his reputation for daring and military brilliance had reached far beyond Italy's shores, and President Abraham Lincoln tried to enlist his help in the U.S. Civil War. Garibaldi was offered a commission as a general in the Union army. The offer met with Garibaldi's refusal when Lincoln could not grant the Italian's rather surprising demands to be made commander in chief for all Northern forces and that slavery be immediately outlawed. Perhaps the greatest tribute to Garibaldi was his triumphal visit to England in 1864. Never before in history had anyone drawn such enthusiastic and spontaneous crowds as those that cheered Garibaldi on the streets of London.

Perhaps this is why Garibaldi found it difficult to lay down his sword for good. Although he professed to be a peace-loving man, he seemed incapable of standing aside whenever there was a battle to be fought. Consequently, even in his declining years, he repeatedly answered the call to arms. The first time was in 1862. Unhappy with the course of events in the Papal States, Garibaldi marched on Rome, was badly wounded at the Battle of Aspromonte, and then was taken prisoner. Granted amnesty by King Victor Emmanuel, Garibaldi returned to Caprera to recover from his wound, which left him lame. He returned to the battlefield in 1866 to fight against the Austrians, who still controlled Venetia. This brief war ended with Venetia finally being ceded to Italy. In 1867, he led still another

An 1871 cover of *Harper's Weekly* magazine depicted Garibaldi and King Victor Emmanuel guiding a figure of Italy through the flames of war. The crests surrounding the illustration represent the recently united Italian provinces.

assault on the Papal States, which he so much wanted to seize from the pope's dominion.

After raising a stir at a conference held by the International League of Peace and Liberty in Geneva, Switzerland, Garibaldi was at the peak of his idealism. He was convinced that there was a popular demand to overthrow the pope's government. But the man who had referred to the papacy as "the negation of God" and considered himself the champion of "truth and reason" had deceived himself. He proceeded toward inevitable defeat at Mentana, mistakenly thinking the Italian government would shield and support him. The government had only

Garibaldi received a rousing welcome from crowds at the newly built Crystal Palace during his 1864 tour of England. British government officials, however, declined to meet with him for fear of offending their French allies.

THE BETTMANN ARCHIVE/BBC HULTON

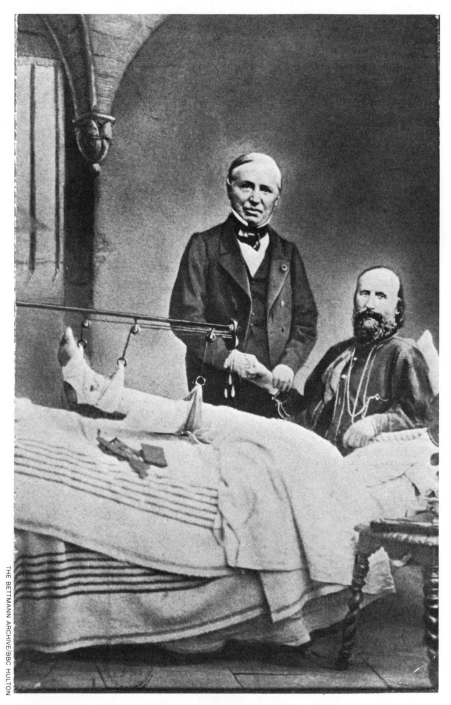

Garibaldi was photographed in 1862 with the English
physician who attended his wound after Aspromonte.
That failed campaign against the Papal States demonstrated his continued willingness to champion causes
of "truth and reason."

recognized that Garibaldi's popularity made it necessary to communicate with him.

His march on Rome made contact with papal and French forces on November 3. The enemy's losses amounted to only a handful, and Garibaldi managed a quick getaway, but 1,600 of his volunteers were taken prisoner in the fiasco. After this defeat he was placed under arrest, only to be released once again to return to Caprera.

Garibaldi's final campaign was in 1870, when, incredibly, he went to the aid of France during the Franco-Prussian War. No matter that the French had often been his mortal enemy. He believed they were being wronged by Prussia and fought on their behalf. The French, in appreciation for his minor but distinguished contribution, elected him to the National Assembly at Bordeaux.

It was rheumatism and the effects of his many wounds, not diminished fervor, that forced Gari-

In his last years, Garibaldi had become an invalid from the effects of his many wounds. He kept up an interest in revolutionary and political events until his death at age 74.

ALINARI, FLORENCE

baldi into retirement at last. Nonetheless, he continued to receive visitors and to keep abreast of foreign events. A revolutionary to the end, he espoused socialism toward the end of his life, although Karl Marx, the father of modern socialist theory, rejected his support.

As early as 1860, Garibaldi had tried to annul his marriage to Marchesina Raimondi, but he met with resistance to his request from both the king and Prime Minister Cairoli. Finally, shortly before his death, the annulment was granted, and he married Francesca Armosino.

The old warrior was 74 when he died on June 2, 1882. Still living in his little white cottage on the island of Caprera, he liked to sit on his bed, propped up with pillows. There he would watch the sea and feed the birds that often flew to his windowsill. The evening he died, two finches came to the window and chirped loudly for their supper. As the attendants moved to shoo them away, Garibaldi stopped them. "Let the birds come in," he whispered, "and always feed them when I am gone."

Garibaldi's tomb on the island of Caprera, photographed in the late 1800s. Francesca Armosino Garibaldi, his third wife, wears the traditional heavy black garb of Italian widows.

8

Garibaldi in Retrospect

Historians agree that the unification of Italy was largely the work of four individuals — Cavour, Mazzini, Victor Emmanuel, and Garibaldi. Each had a role. Cavour, the creative genius and string puller behind the unification effort, was a calculating politician who manipulated people and events to suit what some of his critics have regarded as his own selfish interests. It seems plausible to say that he wanted as much as anyone to unify Italy, but not at the price of revolution — a circumstance that could tear down Italy's traditional and rigid social hierarchy. Mazzini, an impractical visionary, gave the Risorgimento its intellectual force and validity. At the same time, while Mazzini labored at his often vague notions of Italian republicanism, he abhorred radical reforms, and, in times requiring bold action, was indecisive. King Victor Emmanuel, a nationalist at heart, had the wisdom to work with the many conflicting forces within Italy to achieve unification.

Each of these men was important to the success of the Risorgimento, but it would have been impossible without Garibaldi. This ardent nationalist and champion of the common man was the heart and soul of the unification effort. Only he was able to inspire peasants, businessmen, and students alike to sacrifice their lives for such an elusive ideal as Italian unification.

With all his failings, Giuseppe Garibaldi is firmly fixed among the great men of the 19th century.
—DENIS MACK SMITH
British historian

A major exhibit at the 1884 Italian Exposition in Turin was devoted to memorabilia of the Risorgimento. Garibaldi is the central figure; to his left are the boots he wore at Aspromonte, and the poncho, cap, and bandanna he wore at the battle for Palermo.

THE BETTMANN ARCHIVE

Yet even today, more than a century after his death, it is difficult to explain how such a simple, unpretentious man could have accomplished so much with so little. He was no intellectual or politician; he was a soldier. But what a soldier! It was his victories on the field of battle that made unification a reality.

Nonetheless, a disciplined soldier he was not. The drill field bored him. He neither knew nor cared about such military fundamentals as organization and logistics. His tactics were uncomplicated. His basic strategy was simply to make a decision and stick to it, come what may, for he had tremendous self-confidence. And it was this self-confidence — combined with an utter disregard for his own safety — that inspired those around him to herculean efforts.

Although he knew little about military tactics and strategy, he possessed an innate ability to assess a situation and react correctly. According to one of his volunteers, "Garibaldi, on the approach of a foe, would ride up to a culminating point in the landscape, survey the ground for hours with the spyglass in brooding silence, and come down with a swoop on the enemy, acting upon some well-contrived combination of movements by which advantage had been taken of all circumstances in his favor."

His self-effacing humility and lack of selfish ambition also contributed to his success. Rewards and honors were his for the taking, but these never interested him. In fact, he was almost monastic in his personal wants and behavior and died as poor and humble as he lived. Even his enemies could not fault his sincerity and generosity. But the more he disdained personal gain, the greater became his image as a patriot and savior. To the people of Italy he seemed godly or saintly, and mothers begged him to bless their babies. One of his most infatuated biographers, British historian G. M. Trevelyan, viewed Garibaldi's life "as the most poetical of all true stories."

His lack of military training, however, could also be a weakness. Because he depended almost entirely

He was a man who seemed to preach peace even in the middle of battle, who created a nation with a small group of soldiers, who founded a monarchy though proclaiming himself a republican.
—ALFREDO ORIANI
Italian writer, on Garibaldi

ALDO DURAZZI, ROME

Even Garibaldi's enemies could not fault his inspiring selflessness. The chief message of his life signaled that idealism and patriotism can triumph over impossible odds.

on bayonet charges and raw courage when attacking his opponent, he sometimes needlessly sacrificed the lives of his blindly loyal volunteers. Rather than take the time to probe for an enemy's weaknesses, he often resorted to suicidal frontal attacks, using small detachments of lightly armed men. As a result, he lost some of his finest officers and could well have been killed himself had not providence and luck been his constant companions.

Whatever his faults, there is no doubt that Garibaldi was a sincere patriot and dedicated nationalist. He was also an avowed radical and tireless revolutionary, which helps to explain his support of socialism in his last years. However, as early as 1860 various social issues won his concern and involvement. He actively opposed the death penalty and went so far as to proclaim, "The future greatness of Italy lies in particular with the working-classes."

His image remained both heroic and vague, causing both Italian right-wing extremists (principally

ART RESOURCE

Every major city in modern Italy features a monument to Garibaldi, such as this one, in Venice. His vision of a liberated, unified nation was the basis for his heroic achievements.

the fascists led by Italian dictator Benito Mussolini) and communists to claim Garibaldi for themselves. Although he called himself a socialist, Garibaldi was no ideologue; he did not grasp, nor was he drawn to, complex political and economic notions. His life's work had resulted from his passionate belief in freedom and fair play. He was seldom careful enough to discern what programs would best achieve them. What little he understood about socialism — its emphasis on social equality, broad-based reform, and collective ownership — must have seemed to him in line with his humanitarian principles.

Such efforts, and his brief dictatorship in Sicily, notwithstanding, Garibaldi was not a supporter of fascist politics or of communism. He was a nationalist. Italian nationalism, he himself said, had been "the cult and religion [of his] entire life." He wanted to liberate people, not enslave them either politically or intellectually. This is why Garibaldi has earned such an eminent place in world history.

THE BETTMANN ARCHIVE

During his lifetime, Garibaldi attracted a fanatical devotion that was not limited to his fellow countrymen; he was for some years the most widely admired public figure in the world.

Further Reading

Bowle, John. *Politics and Opinion in the Nineteenth Century.* London: Oxford Galaxy, 1954.

Leeds, Christopher. *The Unification of Italy.* New York: Putnam's, 1974.

May, Arthur J. *The Age of Metternich 1814–1848.* New York: Holt, Rinehart, and Winston, 1963.

Rich, Norman. *The Age of Nationalism and Reform.* New York: Norton, 1970.

Ridley, Jasper. *Garibaldi.* New York: Viking, 1976.

Smith, Denis Mack. *Garibaldi: A Great Life in Brief.* New York: Knopf, 1956.

———. *Garibaldi: Great Lives Observed.* Englewood Cliffs, NJ: Prentice-Hall, 1969.

———. *Making of Italy, 1796–1870.* London: Walker, 1968.

Whyte, Arthur J. *The Evolution of Modern Italy.* New York: Norton, 1959.

Chronology

July 4, 1807	Giuseppe Garibaldi is born in Nice, France
1823–34	Sails with merchant navy; eventually becomes captain
1834	Conspires with Giuseppe Mazzini's supporters in an unsuccessful nationalist revolution; flees to France after he is condemned to death in Italy
Nov. 1835	Arrives in Rio de Janeiro, Brazil
1836–40	Fights in Brazilian civil war
1842	Becomes commander of Uruguayan fleet in war with Argentina
1848	Widespread revolution threatens Europe's ruling houses Garibaldi leads a group of Red Shirts to Italy
Aug. 13, 1848	Issues the Castelletto Manifesto attacking King Charles Albert's truce with Austria
1849	Fights for the Roman Republic and then leads retreat to San Marino Death of Garibaldi's wife, Anita
1850	Escapes to the United States
1854	Returns to Italy
1859	Appointed major general in Sardinian army; leads the Alpine Rifles against the Austrians
May–Oct. 1860	Leads a successful expedition to liberate Sicily and southern Italy from Bourbon rule
Oct. 26, 1860	Meets King Victor Emmanuel and agrees to cede southern Italy to the king to form a united Italy
1864	Visits England, where he is given an enthusiastic reception
1866	Leads a group of volunteers who liberate Venetia from Austrian rule
1867	Heads an abortive expedition to end papal control of Rome
1870	Fights for France in Franco-Prussian War
June 2, 1882	Dies at his cottage on the island of Caprera

Index

Aguiar, 49, 53, 54, 55, 58

Argentina, 38, 39

Austrian Empire, 14, 27, 28, 47, 51, 52, 61, 73, 74, 79

Black Sea, 26

Bonaparte, Prince Napoleon ("Plon-Plon"), 74

Bonnet, Giacomo, 65, 66

Bourbons, the, 15, 16, 28, 86, 87, 88, 89, 90, 92

Bovi, Major, 67

Brazil, 37, 38, 39

Buonarotti, Philippe, 30

Byron, Lord (George Gordon), 30, 31

Cacciatore delle Alpi (the Alpine Rifles), 78, 79, 83

Cairoli, Benedetto, 84

Calabria, 47

Calatafimi, 13, 17, 19, 85, 86

Caprera, 70, 95, 96, 97, 100, 101

Carbonari ("charcoal burners"), 29, 30, 31

"Castelleto Manifesto," 50

Cavour, Count Camillo Benso di, 72, 73, 74, 75, 77, 78, 79, 80, 81, 91, 103

Charles Albert, king of Piedmont, 47, 49, 51, 66

Cialdini, Enrico, 81

Congress of Vienna, 27, 28

Constituent Assembly, 58

Crimean War, 73, 74, 81

Crispi, Francesco, 79

Cucelli, 67

Culiolo, Giovanni ("Leggero"), 64, 65, 67

Custozza, Battle of, 49

"Death Angle," 55

Fanti, Manfredo, 83

Farini, Luigi Carlo, 73, 83

fascism, 107

feudalism, 16

"Final Act," 28

"Five Glorious Days, the," 49

France, 14, 23, 47, 52, 61, 73, 82, 83

Franco-Prussian War, 100

Franz Joseph II, emperor of Austria, 47, 81

French Revolution, 27

Garibaldi, Anita Ribeiro da Silva (first wife) death, 63, 64, 65, 67
in Nice, 48, 49, 51
meeting with Garibaldi, 41

rejoins Garibaldi, 57, 59

Garibaldi, Domenici (father), 24

Garibaldi, Francesca Armosino (third wife), 101

Garibaldi, Giuseppe
death, 101
defense of Rome, 52–59
exile in South America, 33, 35, 36, 37, 43
first marriage, 42
first return to Italy, 48, 49
second exile, 67
second marriage, 72
second return, 75
in Sicily, 83–91, 107
third marriage, 101
Young Italy and, 31, 32, 36, 37
youth, 23, 24, 25, 27

Garibaldi, Marchesina Giuseppina Raimondi (second wife), 72, 101

Garibaldi, Menotti (oldest son), 42, 70, 95

Garibaldi, Ricciotti (son), 45

Garibaldi, Rosita (daughter), 45

Garibaldi, Teresita (daughter), 45

Garibaldini, 57, 64, 66, 89, 90

Garibaldinismo, 51

"Garibaldi's Hymn" (Mercantini), 18, 21

gauchos, 38, 45

Geneva, Switzerland, 98

Genoa, 84

German Confederation, 27

Germany, 27

Gilbraltar, 67

Giovine Italia see Young Italy

Habsburg, house of, 14, 15, 16, 28, 47

Herzen, Aleksandr, 69

Il Risorgimento (newspaper), 73

International League of Peace and Liberty, the, 98

Italian Legion, 43, 44, 45

Laguna, Brazil, 39, 40

Lincoln, Abraham, 96

Lombardy, province of, 15, 28, 49, 74, 82

London, 45, 68, 69, 70

Louis-Philippe, king of France, 47

Lucca, 15

Magenta, Battle of, 79

Marches, the, 15

Marsala, 84
Marseilles, 35
Martini della Torre, Maria, 72
Marx, Karl, 31, 101
Mazzini, Giuseppe, 31, 33, 45, 47, 51, 52,
    53, 54, 56, 69, 72, 75, 77, 83, 103
Mediterranean Sea, 26
Menotti, Ciro, 31
Meucci, 68
Milan, 49
Milazzo, Battle of, 89
Modena, 15, 28, 74
Montevideo, Uruguay, 42, 44, 48, 57, 59, 66
Mussolini, Benito, 107
Naples, city of, 52, 61, 62, 82, 89
Naples, kingdom of see Two Sicilies, kingdom
    of the
Napoleon I, 14, 23, 28
Napoleon III, emperor of France, 74, 79, 81
Napoleonic wars, 14
Neapolitan army, 21, 53, 84, 85, 89, 90
New York, 67
Nice, 23, 25, 27, 32, 48, 49, 51, 57, 67, 83
Palermo, 85, 86, 87, 88
Papal States, the, 15, 29, 51, 74, 83, 92, 97,
    98
Parma, 15, 28, 74
Peru, 68
Piedmont, kingdom of see Sardinia, kingdom
    of
Piedmontese flag, 17, 36
Pio Nono see Pius IX
Piscane, Carlo, 75
Pius VII, 29
Pius IX (Pio Nono), 48, 51, 81
Plombières, agreement of, 73, 74
populism, 69
Portugal, 36
Prussia, 100
Red Shirts, 19, 20, 21, 44, 48, 49, 58, 72,
    84, 85, 89, 93
Republic of Rome, 52, 53, 59, 61
Republican army, 59
Ricasoli, Baron Bettino, 83
Ricciotti, Nicola, 47
Rio de Janeiro, 36
Risorgimento, 17, 27, 35, 72, 95, 103
Roberts, Emma, 70

Romagna, 15
Roman Empire, 13, 14
Rome, 15, 48, 51, 52, 59, 61, 63, 64, 74
Rossi, Pellegrino Luigi Eduardo, 52
Russians, 73
Saint-Simon, Claude-Henri de Rouvray, 31,
    32
Saint-Simonians, 31, 32
St. Peter's Basilica, 59
San Marino, 63
San Mastino, Battle of see Solferino, Battle of
Sardinia, kingdom of (Piedmont, kingdom of),
    15, 28, 32, 34, 50, 65, 74, 80, 81, 82,
    90, 95
Sardinian army, 77
Savoy, house of, 74, 81, 83
Second Republic (of France), 47
secret societies, 29
Sicily, 13, 28, 82, 83, 84, 85, 86, 87, 89, 91,
    92, 107
Smith, Denis Mack, 91
socialism, 101, 105, 107
Solferino, 81
Solferino, Battle of, 78, 79, 81
South America, 35, 78
Spain, 36, 52, 61
Staten Island, 68
Switzerland, 33
Tangier, 67
"Thousand, The," 17, 19, 84, 85, 92,
    95
Tunis, 67
Turin, 58, 75, 77, 92
Tuscany, 15, 28, 83
Two Sicilies, kingdom of the, (Naples,
    kingdom of), 13, 16, 28, 29, 47, 52,
    74, 89, 90, 92
Tyrrhenian Sea, 15
Umbria, 15
Union army, 96
United States, 67, 69
Uruguay, 39, 44, 45, 48
Uruguayan navy, 43
U.S. Civil War, 96
Venetia, province of, 15, 28, 49, 74, 97
Venice, 62, 64
Victor Emmanuel II, 47, 66, 72, 73, 77, 78,
    81, 82, 83, 92, 93, 95, 97, 103

Villa Corsini, 52, 54
Villafranca, Treaty of, 81
von Metternich, Klemens, 27, 29, 49

von Schwartz, Maria Espérance, 70
Waterloo, Battle of, 28
Young Italy, 31, 32, 36, 37

Herman J. Viola received his B.A. and M.A. from Marquette University and his Ph.D. from Indiana University. He has been assistant editor of the *Indiana Magazine of History* and the editor of *Prologue: The Journal of the National Archives*, which he founded in 1968. Since 1972, Dr. Viola has served as director of the National Anthropological Archives at the Smithsonian Institution. His major publications include *Thomas L. McKenney* (1974), *The Indian Legacy of Charles Bird King* (1976), *Diplomats in Buckskin* (1981), and the *National Archives of the United States*. He is the author of *Andrew Jackson* in the Chelsea House series WORLD LEADERS   PAST & PRESENT.

Susan P. Viola received her B.A. from Marquette University and her M.A. in library science from the Catholic University. Since 1980 she has been a librarian at the Madeira School in Greenway, Virginia.

Arthur M. Schlesinger, jr., taught history at Harvard for many years and is currently Albert Schweitzer Professor of the Humanities at City University of New York. He is the author of numerous highly praised works in American history and has twice been awarded the Pulitzer Prize. He served in the White House as special assistant to Presidents Kennedy and Johnson.